Fidel Castro and Che Guevara: The Legen

By Charles River Ed

About Charles River Editors

Charles River Editors was founded by Harvard and MIT alumni to provide superior editing and original writing services, with the expertise to create digital content for publishers across a vast range of subject matter. In addition to providing original digital content for third party publishers, Charles River Editors republishes civilization's greatest literary works, bringing them to a new generation via ebooks.

Introduction

Fidel Castro (1924-)

"Men do not shape destiny. Destiny produces the man for the hour." – Fidel Castro, 1959.

Fidel Castro is one of the most influential and controversial men of the last 50 years, equally revered and reviled by people across the globe. To the West, Castro has long been one of the prominent faces of Communism, and the main reason Cuba has been ostracized by many liberal democracies, particularly the United States. On the other hand, Castro has been admired by those who despised capitalism, and despite the fact the political platform Castro advocated has been almost universally repudiated and only maintains a weak hold even in Cuba, Castro's Marxist-leaning writings and speeches have influenced other leaders across the globe, from Hugo Chavez to Nelson Mandela.

Although his health has been poor for several years, and rumors relentlessly abound about his imminent demise, Castro continues to be the face of Cuba, for better and worse. But while everybody is at least partially familiar with his leadership of the Cuban Revolution and Cuba itself, far fewer are familiar with Castro's past and the vision he had for himself. *Fidel Castro and Che Guevara* chronicles the life, work and revolutions Castro was involved in, while analyzing the controversies and legacy he left in his wake. Along with pictures of important people, places, and events in his life, you will learn about Fidel like you never have before.

Che Guevara (1928-1967)

"The revolution is not an apple that falls when it is ripe. You have to make it fall." – Che Guevara

Ernesto Guevara de la Serna, known to the world as Che, has led two lives. In the first of these lives, the Argentine-born revolutionary was a remarkable and flawed doctor-turned-guerilla who left behind a highly controversial political legacy. In the second, he was – and is – first and foremost an image. Specifically, he is one particular image in which he appears as a wavy-haired, bearded young man with a beret and an intense gaze. The photograph, entitled Guerrillero Heroico and taken on March 5, 1960 by Cuban photographer Alberto Korda, is said to be the most reproduced image in the history of photography. Although Che's face, as captured by Korda, first achieved its global iconic status during the student revolts of the 1960s, it has subsequently reappeared again and again as a branding device for a wide array of products. Korda himself brought a copyright lawsuit against Smirnoff Vodka for using Guerillero Heroico in an advertising campaign, and since Korda's 2001 death his daughter has gone to court with several other companies. There is little market for the type of revolution that Che advocated and pursued, but the aura of rebellion that his image exudes still carries a notable sway.

The current status of Che Guevara, then, is paradoxical. The political platform he advocated as a communist revolutionary has been almost universally repudiated and only maintains a weak hold even in Cuba, the country where he exercised the greatest impact. The violent struggles he spearheaded in the Congo and Bolivia look at best quixotic and at worst foolish and pointlessly destructive. Yet Che is in no danger of being forgotten, mainly due to the persistent appeal of a decontextualized image. Most ironically of all, his image is frequently deployed to the direct economic benefit of the kinds of multinational corporations whose power he hoped to obliterate. In contrast to the quaint and hoary air that now surrounds other revolutionaries like Lenin, Mao, and even Fidel Castro, Che has managed to maintain a youthful glamour and allure in the post-Cold War world. And although any future revolutionary movements in an increasingly urbanized world are unlikely to look much like the peasant insurgencies Che led and theorized, it is likely that their leaders will continue to invoke his image and his example.

When considered as a political figure, Che is most notable for his unwavering commitment to the ideals and goals that motivated him. Even his fiercest critics would never accuse him of cynicism, and his lack of willingness to compromise probably did him significant damage and shortened his life. Unusually among revolutionary leaders and in stark contrast to his compañero Castro, Che seemed to have no strong attachment to power. Having reached the pinnacle of his authority as the second-in-command of the new revolutionary Cuba and having occupied several prominent government positions, he preferred to leave Cuba and take part in obscure and ultimately hopeless struggles in remote corners of Africa and South America. He was as vulnerable as any of the far less famous men he fought with, and he suffered the same fate as many of them. Depending on who's asked, his dogged and fierce commitment may be described as admirable idealism or as deranged dogmatism.

Fidel Castro and Che Guevara chronicles the world's most famous revolutionary's life, examining both his writings and the revolutions he led, but it also humanizes the guerrilla leader and looks at the controversies and legacy he left in his wake. Along with pictures of important people, places, and events in his life, you will learn about Che like you never have before.

Che and Fidel, photographed by Alberto Korda in 1961.

Chapter 1: Che's Origins and Early Years

"One has to grow hard but without ever losing tenderness." - Che

Che (far left) as a teenager

Ernesto Guevara de la Serna was the first child born to Ernesto Guevara Lynch and Celia de la Serna Llosa, who were both descended from early Spanish settlers in Argentina, although his father was also descended from more recent Irish immigrants. The spirit of adventure remained strong in the family beyond the initial pioneer generation. Several of Che's ancestors on both sides had escaped the political tumult of 19th century Argentina to seek their fortune in the California gold rush of 1849, and his paternal grandfather Roberto had been born in California. Not long before their son's birth, the newly married couple had perpetuated the family's pioneering tradition by moving from Buenos Aires to the remote and hot Misiones region of Northern Argentina. Guevara Lynch invested an inheritance in a purchase of land for the cultivation of *yerba mate*, the plant used to make *mate*, a popular tea consumed in the southern reaches of South America. However, the conditions in Misiones, a sparsely populated tropical region, were harsh and rustic enough to oblige the couple to return to the nearest large city, Rosario, for the birth of their child.

Ernesto was born in Rosario on May 14, 1928, but because Celia had become pregnant before her wedding to Guevara Lynch, the couple arranged to have the birth certificate falsified to read June 14, and they even waited a month before informing their families in Buenos Aires of the boy's arrival. After his birth, the family returned to Misiones, where they remained until late 1929. With Celia pregnant a second time and Guevara Lynch needing to conduct some business in the capital, they traveled to Buenos Aires. Although they intended to return to the *mate* plantation, various circumstances got in the way and it proved more convenient to remain in the city – and there they remained until 1932. During this time, Celia gave birth to a third child, and young Ernesto began to have the severe asthma attacks that would continue to afflict him throughout his life.

Surprisingly for a man who would later survive long stretches in the harshest wilderness conditions, Ernesto proved to have highly delicate health, and his proneness to debilitating asthma finally prompted the family to move again, this time to the drier climate of the interior Córdoba region. It was here that the family would remain for the remainder of Ernesto's childhood, living first in the spa town of Alta Gracia and later in the city of Córdoba itself. Although he continued to be afflicted by asthma, Ernesto quickly became an adventurous child prone to risk-seeking. Noting his son's restless nature, Guevara Lynch proudly boasted that "the first thing to note is that in my son's veins flowed the blood of the Irish rebels."

Ernesto also showed his first curiosity about politics during his childhood years in Córdoba. The region saw a notable influx of refugees from the Spanish Civil War in the late 1930s and early 1940s, supporters of the Republic who had fled Franco's victorious forces, and Ernesto Guevara Lynch befriended a number of them and invited them to the house. Ernesto and Celia also became vocal supporters of the Allied powers in World War II, and both father and son went on spying expeditions in some of the German communities in and around Córdoba, where it was suggested that clandestine pro-Nazi organizations had been operating.

Ernesto's high school years saw him become more academically adept and intellectually curious, with his interests ranging from chess to poetry, but he remained something of a thrill-seeker. He became an enthusiastic rugby player known by his teammates for his frenzied style of play, and it was on his rugby team that he met Alberto Granado, a close friend with whom he would later travel extensively.

Granado (left) and Che in 1952

Ernesto was a voracious reader from a young age, and he began to steep himself in the classics of European literature as well as Latin American literature. It was from reading such authors as the Guatemalan Miguel Ángel Asturias and the Peruvian Ciro Alegría that he first became vividly aware of some of the countries he would later travel in. In school, he began to excel in particular in the sciences, but at the same time he developed a strong curiosity about philosophy through a course that he took, and he began to compose his own "philosophical dictionaries" that outlined major concepts and arguments. It was during this time that he first read some of the works of Marx and Engels, although he did not initially show any particular devotion to Marxism. A declassified C.I.A. document from 1958 noted how well read Che was and concluded, "Che is fairly intellectual for a Latino."

If Ernesto's first political awareness came from his interest in the events of the Spanish Civil War and the rise of the Nazis in Germany, the political scene in Argentina was itself quite tumultuous during his early years. While the Argentine governments of the 1930s were for the most part short-lived and ineffectual, the early 1940s saw the rise of a figure who would exercise an outsized influence on the country for decades to come: Juan Domingo Perón. An army colonel, Perón first rose to prominence as a minister of labor under the military junta that took power in a coup in 1943. Perón successfully channeled the nationalist sentiments of the poorer sectors of the Argentine population, and managed to gain a large backing among the labor movement as well as much of the army. His denunciations of the oligarchy and of foreign capitalists alarmed many of the more conservative military officers, but their attempt to silence him through imprisonment in 1945 backfired and led to a mass movement demanding his release. When elections were held in 1946, Perón won a resounding victory, and he expanded his appeal to the working class through a wide array of social programs organized mainly by his charismatic wife, Eva Duarte Perón, a former actress. "Evita" would become a lightning rod in Argentine politics, adored by many of the poorest Argentines and despised by the traditional oligarchy and a large portion of the middle class.

Peron

The Guevaras and de la Sernas, both old and prosperous clans, belonged to the sector of Argentine society most hostile to Juan and Eva Perón, and Ernesto did not show any great enthusiasm for the new regime. There was much to be suspicious of, particularly since Perón had shown a public enthusiasm for Italian fascism and was widely assumed to have Nazi sympathies as well. Although he relied heavily on patronage networks to preserve and consolidate his hold on power, Perón also imprisoned his opponents and used heavy-handed tactics against opposition demonstrators, leading some to fear that a one-party police state was just around the corner.

Ernesto did not take active part in any of the political conflicts of the period and avoided aligning himself with any particular faction, but Perón's example likely proved important to his political education in two ways. First, Perón's politically successful platform of anti-imperialism and social justice provided a prototype for the kind of politics Ernesto would ultimately make his own, even though Perón's ideals were those of military nationalism and not communism (in fact, communists were severely persecuted in Perón's Argentina). Second, as biographer John Lee Anderson has noted, Perón demonstrated to him that "[w]hat was required to make political headway in a place such as Argentina was strong leadership and a willingness to use force to meet one's goals."

For the most part, though, Ernesto showed no inclination to play a direct role in politics, and he refused invitations from various friends to join politically oriented groups. On the other hand, his own struggles with asthma and grandmother's death around the end of his high school years caused him to discard his initial plan of studying engineering in favor of medicine, remarking that he thought he could make more of a difference as a doctor than as an engineer. In May 1947, he moved with his entire family back to Buenos Aires, after having lived in Córdoba region for fifteen years, and soon after he was accepted at the medical school of the University of Buenos Aires. Alongside his studies, he began working at an allergy clinic that had pioneered a new asthma treatment. He was listed as co-author for some of the published research that came out of the clinic, and for a time he considered becoming an asthma researcher. While in medical school, he began to develop a passion for travel that took him on weekend hitchhiking, walking, and cycling trips to various other parts of Argentina. He also extended his readings of Marx, Engels, and Lenin, but his interests still did not pass beyond an intellectual curiosity.

Che in 1951

On a particularly long bicycle trip to the North of Argentina, Che stopped in Córdoba and visited his friend Alberto Granado, who had studied biochemistry and was now working at a leprosy clinic. He then continued nearly as far as the border with Bolivia, where he witnessed a very different Argentina than the one he had known: poor, agrarian, and predominantly indigenous. The trip clearly made an enormous impression on him, and in 1952, when he was only a handful of exams away from finishing, he and Granado would set out on an epic trip toward the northern reaches of the continent, with the goal of seeing this "other" Latin America Ernesto had glimpsed near the Bolivian border. They also hoped to reach the United States, the colossus of the North that Ernesto already held responsible for many of Latin America's most enduring problems. They set out from Córdoba on January 4, 1952, on Alberto's motorcycle, nicknamed La Poderosa. The trip would radically alter both of their lives.

Chapter 2: Che's Early Travels and Political Awakening

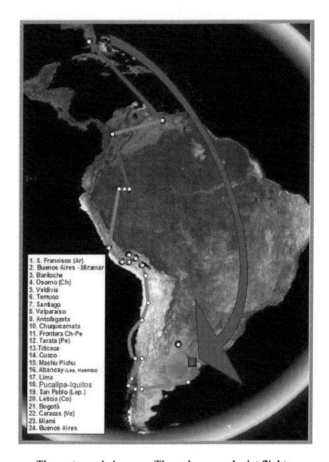

1. S. Francisco (Ar)
2. Buenos Aires - Miramar
3. Bariloche
4. Osorno (Ch)
5. Valdivia
6. Temuco
7. Santiago
8. Valparaiso
9. Antofagasta
10. Chuquicamata
11. Frontera Ch-Pe
12. Tarata (Pe)
13. Titicaca
14. Cuzco
15. Machu Pichu
16. Abancay (Lep. Huambo)
17. Lima
18. Pucallpa-Iquitos
19. San Pablo (Lep.)
20. Leticia (Co)
21. Bogotá
22. Caracas (Ve)
23. Miami
24. Buenos Aires

The motorcycle journey. The red arrows depict flights.

"This isn't a tale of derring-do, nor is it merely some kind of 'cynical account'; it isn't meant to be, at least. It's a chunk of two lives running parallel for a while, with common aspirations and similar dreams. In nine months a man can think a lot of thoughts, from the height of philosophical conjecture to the most abject longing for a bowl of soup – in perfect harmony with the state of his stomach. And if, at the same time, he's a bit of an adventurer, he could have experiences which might interest other people and his random account would read something like this diary." – The introduction to Che's *Motorcycle Diaries*

At the beginning of a trip that would later be romanticized, dramatized, and endlessly written about, Ernesto and Alberto first headed south towards Argentine Patagonia, but they first stopped in the coastal resort of Miramar to visit Chichina, Ernesto's girlfriend. Chichina was the daughter of a wealthy family that disapproved of the young man, an obstacle that only seemed to heighten his determination. His goal on the visit was to persuade the young woman to wait for him until after he returned from the long journey, with the presumable intention of marrying her afterwards. While she did give him the promise he sought, she would later retract it in a message sent to him while on the road. The end of their relationship would later help persuade Ernesto that, other than the completion of medical school, there was nothing to keep him in Argentina. But for the moment, when Ernesto was about to leave Miramar, he still had some sense of a more conventional path than he would ultimately take: a medical career, marriage, and a safe and comfortable life in the country of his birth.

Already on the initial Patagonian stretch of the trip, the two adventurers realized their money was running out and began to develop the strategies they would use throughout the trip to keep their expenses low. For one, they presented themselves as doctors wherever they went and offered their services where they could be useful. On top of that, they used their charm to solicit the hospitality of people they met along the way. The first stage of their trajectory took them through the spectacular lake district on the Argentine side of the Andean range, and then across a mountain lake into Chile. In several towns in the south of Chile, they stepped up their attempts to publicize their presence by visiting newspaper offices, and in both Valdivia and Temuco the local newspapers ran articles about them introducing them as Argentine doctors with an expertise in leprology. The ploy succeeded in obtaining room and board in several places, until they met some Chilean doctors who informed them that Chile's only leper colony was on the South Pacific territory of Easter Island. This persuaded them, for a time, that their next port of call should be the exotic and faraway Easter Island, but they later discovered that ships heading there were so irregularly scheduled that they would have to wait several months to depart.

Che and La Poderosa

Alberto's motorcycle began to give them mechanical trouble in Chile, and it was not long before they were forced to abandon "La Poderosa" and continue their journey by other means. Not long after arriving at the port of Valparaíso, they managed to sneak on board a cargo ship and hide in a latrine until after the ship was out at sea. When the captain discovered the pair, he let them remain on board in exchange for odd jobs in the kitchen and on the cleaning crew. The ship took them to Antofagasta, where they tried and failed to stow away on another vessel. They then determined to make their way to Peru by land.

Before heading to Peru, the two decided to visit the Chuquicamata copper mine, Chile's largest mine and the source of much of the country's revenue. The operations at Chuquicamata were run by U.S. companies Anaconda and Kenecott, and as a result much of the wealth generated by the mine ended up being funneled out of the country, leading mining unions and left-wing and nationalist leaders to call for the nationalization of the mine. Ernesto and Alberto were evidently aware of this situation when they went to Chuquicamata, and Ernesto's diary reveals that his antipathies for the U.S. owners of the mine were pronounced. In his *Motorcyle Diaries*, Che wrote, "The most important effort that needs to be done is to get rid of the uncomfortable 'Yankee-friend'. It is especially at this moment an immense task, because of the great amount of dollars they have invested here and the convenience of using economical pressure whenever they believe their interests are being threatened."

The two travelers also encountered a man and his wife who were also hitchhiking near the mine. The man revealed that he was a miner who had been fired from his job because of his membership in Chile's Communist Party. Ernesto described the couple in his diary as "a live representation of the proletariat of any part of the world," language suggesting that his experiences were strengthening Ernesto's incipient Marxist leanings.

Their subsequent travels in Peru contributed further to the political formation of the future Che. They entered the country in the high Andean region surrounding Lake Titicaca, an area mainly populated by indigenous peoples who spoke Quechua and Aymara. While they expressed sympathy with the plight of the impoverished masses, they benefited throughout the trip from the country's deeply ingrained ethnic hierarchies: as two white Argentines, they were able to rely on the hospitality of the Guardia Civil, Peru's national police force. When they arrived at Guardia Civil posts and announced themselves as "Argentine doctors," they were treated with a deference and generosity that the locals never enjoyed from the authorities. Alberto and Ernesto visited the ancient Inca capital of Cuzco, where Ernesto marveled over the remains of Inca architecture upon which it was built. Through a Peruvian doctor they met in Cuzco, the two obtained free passage by train to the ancient citadel of Machu Picchu, which evidently made an enormous impression on both. In addition to rhapsodizing over the splendor of the place and expressing sympathy for the "conquered races" that once ruled Peru, Ernesto expressed disgust for the American tourists who were already flocking to the site en masse. Before leaving Peru, he wrote in his diary, "I want to link my destiny to that of the poor of this world."

Upon their return to Cuzco, the doctor who had obtained the train passages to Machu Picchu gave them a letter of introduction that would allow them to volunteer at a nearby leprosarium. There they went, but their time there was cut short by an asthma attack that debilitated Ernesto for several days. Having decided that they needed to go to a hospital, they proceeded onwards towards the capital city of Lima, stopping in the smaller city of Andahuaylas for asthma treatment at the hospital before setting out on a strenuous ten-day journey. Once in the capital, they received money by wire from Argentina and remained for three weeks, enjoying an improved standard of living.

Here Ernesto and Alberto befriended a Lima-based leprologist, Dr. Hugo Pesce, who recommended that they go volunteer in the leprosy treatment center at the Hospital del Guía, which he had established in the Peruvian Amazon. Pesce helped them make arrangements for the trip. Dr. Pesce was also Communist and a disciple of the Peruvian Marxist theoretician José Carlos Mariátegui. As a politically committed physician, he was evidently a figure of admiration for the young Che, who would much later send him an inscribed copy of one of his books from Cuba. Che would write of his time among the lepers, "All the love and caring just consist on coming to them without gloves and medical attire, shaking their hands as any other neighbor and sitting together for a chat about anything or playing football with them." From Lima, they set out over the mountains and then boarded a river boat bound for Iquitos, the capital of Peru's

Amazonian region.

Dr. HUGO PESCE PESCETO

The stay at the Hospital del Guía, which lasted several weeks, was a high point of the trip for both of them. Their presence and work was appreciated, and they enjoyed evening dance parties and afternoon soccer matches with the staff and residents of the hospital. Ernesto celebrated his twenty-fourth birthday at the colony. Soon afterward, they set off on a makeshift raft towards the Colombian Amazon, a border crossing that inaugurated the final stage of their trip.

Their initial destination was the jungle town of Leticia, where they caught an airplane to the capital city of Bogotá. Ernesto was struck by the tense mood of the country, noting in a letter to his mother, "There is more repression of individual freedom here than in any country we've been to, the police patrol the streets carrying rifles and demand your papers every few minutes." The country was still reeling from the riots that had followed the assassination of President Jorge Eliécer Gaitán four years earlier, which had ignited bloody riots. Notably, one of the participants in the riots was the Cuban student Fidel Castro Ruz, who had been visiting Bogotá to attend an anti-imperialist student summit when the assassination occurred. After being harassed by the police, the two young men made a hasty exit, heading toward the neighboring country of Venezuela. In the capital of Caracas, they parted ways, and Alberto would later recall, "I got the impression that Che was saying goodbye to institutional medicine and becoming a doctor of the people." Ernesto, whose asthma had been acting up, decided to end his journey there. Through a business partner of his uncle's, he was able to obtain free passage back to Argentina on a cargo plane, with a stop of several days in Miami – his first visit to the country he already regarded as the root of Latin America's problems. Alberto, meanwhile, found employment in a leprosarium in Venezuela, where he decided to remain indefinitely.

Although his comments about the trip have had far less impact than Che's, Alberto would later note of the journey half a century later, "The trip would not have been as useful and beneficial as it was, as a personal experience, if the motorcycle had held out. This gave us a chance to become familiar with the people. We worked, took on jobs to make money and continue traveling. We hauled merchandise, carried sacks, worked as sailors, cops and doctors."

For Che, however, the journey was transformational. In the course of about 9 months, the pair had covered 5,000 miles through Argentina, Chile, Peru, Ecuador, Colombia, Venezuela, Panama, and to Miami, before Ernesto returned home to Buenos Aires. While treating one woman dying of tuberculosis, Che wrote, "How long this present order, based on the absurd idea of caste, will last is not within my means to answer, but it's time that those who govern spent less time publicizing their own virtues and more money, much more money, funding socially useful works." Che concluded in his account of the journey, "I knew that when the great guiding spirit cleaves humanity into two antagonistic halves, I will be with the

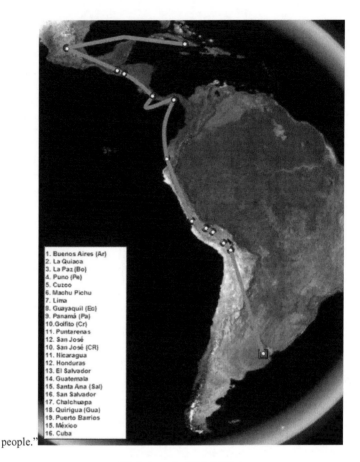

1. Buenos Aires (Ar)
2. La Quiaca
3. La Paz (Bo)
4. Puno (Pe)
5. Cuzco
6. Machu Pichu
7. Lima
8. Guayaquil (Ec)
9. Panamá (Pa)
10. Golfito (Cr)
11. Puntarenas
12. San José
10. San José (CR)
11. Nicaragua
12. Honduras
13. El Salvador
14. Guatemala
15. Santa Ana (Sal)
16. San Salvador
17. Chalchuapa
18. Quirigua (Gua)
19. Puerto Barrios
15. México
16. Cuba

people."

Che's travels, 1953-1956

Upon returning from his trip in July 1952, Guevara wrote in a diary, "I am not the same I was before . . . vagabonding through our 'America' has changed me much more than I thought." He also returned to an Argentina that had changed in his absence, most importantly through the death of Eva Perón at the age of thirty-three. Her disappearance weakened Perón's political hold on the country, even as it strengthened the devotion of a large percentage of the population to the woman and her legacy; in subsequent years, admirers have sought to have her canonized as a saint. Peronism had reached its apogee, and now its survival looked more fragile. Although Perón won reelection in 1952, the opposition was more galvanized than previously, and one could sense mood of implacable conflict that would ultimately lead to the military coup of 1955, which would exile Perón from Argentina for nearly two decades.

At a time when Argentines were taking sides for and against Peronism, one can imagine the newly returned Ernesto, now with a more fully developed political outlook, having thrown himself into the struggle for power that would consume Argentina for the next several decades, culminating in the military dictatorship that ruled from 1976 to 1983. One imagines that he would ultimately have become a confirmed Peronist, given his nationalistic and anti-imperialist outlook – although Peronism was initially rejected by the Argentine socialist left, by the 1970s the most outspoken left-wing groups were supporters of Perón and at least initially applauded his return to power in 1973. But Ernesto did not immerse himself in the simmering cauldron of Argentine politics; his trip had apparently led him to set his sights elsewhere. He remained in Argentina almost exactly one year, long enough to complete the series of exams that qualified him as a doctor and to plan another trip, this time in the company of another old friend from Córdoba, Carlos "Calica" Ferrer.

Ernesto and Calica set out northward with the intention of reaching Alberto in Venezuela. Their ultimate intention, as they were leaving, was to work for a time in Venezuela, and then set out for another continent – both Europe and India were mentioned as destinations. But their first destination this time around was Bolivia, a country Ernesto had not visited with Alberto. It was the first of a series of countries visited on the trip where Ernesto could witness firsthand the conflict between nationalist efforts at reform on one hand and the entrenched power of the traditional oligarchy in an alliance with the neo-imperialist United States, which at the time was endeavoring to augment its hemispheric hegemony by propping up supportive parties and regimes. Bolivia would also be the country where, attempting to participate in a later phase of this struggle, Che would later meet his final fate nearly 15 years later.

In La Paz, the spectacular capital of the country, located at a high elevation and surrounded by snow-capped mountains, the two Argentines met up with family friends who had fled Perón's Argentina. Through them, they were introduced to La Paz high society, interacting with the mainly white oligarchy that controlled a vast percentage of the country's resources, leaving the mostly indigenous masses destitute. Ernesto and Calica had arrived at a dramatic moment, as the oligarchy suddenly felt threatened by the ruling Movimiento Nacionalista Revolucionario, which had seized power in a coup just a year earlier. The government was in the process of implementing an agrarian reform which, among other things, expropriated the massive land holdings of the wealthy landowner class and redistributed the property among the Indian peasantry. As in Peru, Ernesto found the radical social and racial inequalities of the country alarming, especially since he was interacting mainly with people hostile to the reforms, even as he was immediately sympathetic.

The next country visited was again Peru, where Ernesto wished to return to Machu Picchu and Cuzco, still enchanted as he was by the remains of Inca civilization. The trip to the thin-aired heights of the Andes and the humid high jungle region around Machu Picchu again provoked severe asthma attacks, and the relatively bare-bones travel put a strain on the friendship between Ernesto and Calica. Calica complained about the dirt and discomfort to which they were constantly subjected, and in contrast with Ernesto expressed relief when they took refuge in the modern comforts of Lima. In a letter to his mother, Ernesto noted, "Calica keeps cursing the filth and, whenever he treads on one of the innumerable turds lining the streets, he looks at his dirty shoes instead of at the sky or a cathedral outlined in space. He does not smell the intangible and evocative matter of which Cuzco is made, but only the odor of stew and excrement. It's a question of temperament."

Although Ernesto was able to meet with Dr. Pesce there, they decided to leave the country as quickly as possible in part because of the repressive mood they encountered there under the dictatorship of Manuel Odría: Ernesto had had several books confiscated by the Peruvian police on the grounds of their politically subversive content. They proceeded up the coast to Guayaquil, Ecuador's major port city, from whence ships departed daily for dozens of other ports. It was here that Ernesto and Calica, who had turned out not to be as well-suited a traveling companion as Alberto, parted ways. Calica headed on to Venezuela, where he eventually connected with Alberto, while Ernesto decided to head to Central America. His motives were partly political: he knew that Central America was the part of the continent where U.S. influence was felt most oppressively, and wanted to see the state of the region's "banana republics" for himself.

And so he did: his ship docked in Panama, a de facto U.S. fiefdom at the time whose economy was centered around the Panama Canal. He also passed through Nicaragua, ruled by the U.S.-supported dictator Anastasio Somoza. Ernesto's ultimate destination, though, was Guatemala, the one country that had broken with the general pattern of the Central American republics. Under the leadership of the left-leaning army officer Jacobo Arbenz, the country had undertaken a series of agricultural reforms aiming to increase land ownership among the impoverished Indian peasantry and reduce their subjection to large landowners; in the process, the government had expropriated the holdings of the all-powerful United Fruit Company, setting off a conflict with the U.S. that would have deadly consequences for the country. Writing to his aunt in Argentina, Ernesto announced his strong resolve in favor of the country's reform movement: "Along the way, I had the opportunity to pass through the dominions of the United Fruit, convincing me once again of just how terrible these capitalist octopuses are. I have sworn before a picture of the old and mourned comrade Stalin that I won't rest until I see these capitalist octopuses annihilated...In Guatemala I will perfect myself and achieve what I need to be an authentic revolutionary"

As he seemed to anticipate, Ernesto's experience in Guatemala did indeed constitute a kind of political baptism by fire. For one, he got to know revolutionaries in exile from a wide array of Latin American countries who had flocked to Arbenz's Guatemala to help the regime carry out its reforms and take advantage of one of the few governments in the region sympathetic to their causes. It was here that Ernesto had his first contact with exiles from Fulgencio Batista's brutally repressive Cuba, although the Cubans were only one of many groups he came into contact with in Guatemala. During the same period, he also became acquainted with the woman who would become his first wife: Hilda Gadea, a Peruvian member of the outlawed APRA, a left-wing nationalist party that had developed strong ties to Arbenz's governing party in Guatemala. Through Gadea, he became acquainted with members of Arbenz's government, through whom he tried unsuccessfully to obtain work as a doctor in Guatemala's Ministry of Health. He also met an American Marxist professor, Harold White, in this period. Although his general hostility to the U.S. made him initially suspicious of White, the two eventually came to exchange ideas and prognoses for Latin American revolution, and the relationship seemed to help Ernesto confirm his emerging self-identification as a revolutionary Marxist.

Che and Hilda

Whatever doubts may have remained in his mind as to the necessity of revolution vanished with the long-anticipated overthrow of Arbenz's government in a C.I.A.-supported military coup accomplished with logistical help from the Nicaraguan dictator Somoza. The right-wing military man Carlos Castillo Armas was installed in Arbenz's place, and the former president took refuge in the Mexican embassy and instructed his supporters not to take up arms against the new government. Nevertheless, Ernesto attempted to participate in a youth revolt against the new regime, but the rebels were soon persuaded to surrender by the overwhelming superior force of the Guatemalan army. His participation in the aborted rebellion was duly noted by the C.I.A., which opened a file on Ernesto Guevara after the Arbenz overthrow. It was a file that would soon grow into one of the largest they maintained. Lamenting the coup in a letter to a former girlfriend, Ernesto insisted, "If there had been some executions, the government would have maintained the capacity to return the blows."

Arbenz

Shortly after the coup, Hilda Gadea was arrested, and Ernesto took refuge in the Argentine embassy, where he was granted passage into Mexico. Looking back at what had just transpired, Ernesto stated, "The last Latin American revolutionary democracy – that of Jacobo Arbenz – failed as a result of the cold premeditated aggression carried out by the U.S.A. Its visible head was the Secretary of State John Foster Dulles, a man who, through a rare coincidence, was also a stockholder and attorney for the United Fruit Company." He was now firmly convinced that the democratic route to social reform, as implemented by Arbenz, would be a futile pursuit, and that revolution provided the only viable path to genuine change.

He would quickly find occasion to put his new convictions into practice.

Chapter 3: Castro's Early Life

"I feel my belief in sacrifice and struggle getting stronger. I despise the kind of existence that clings to the miserly trifles of comfort and self-interest. I think that a man should not live beyond the age when he begins to deteriorate, when the flame that lighted the brightest moment of his life has weakened." – Fidel Castro, 1953

Fidel Castro was born in Birán, near the town of Mayarí in the Oriente province of Cuba, on August 13, 1926. As destiny would have it, his birthplace was only miles from the Dos Ríos battlefield where the Cuban independence hero, José Martí, had once fought. A journalist and poet, Martí had launched the movement for Cuba's independence from Spain from his exile in

New York City. Martí would become Castro's primary role model, and his eloquently expressed nationalist beliefs would provide the Cuban Revolution's initial ideological inspiration prior to Castro's adoption of Marxism.

Marti

Castro in front of a statue of Mari in Havana, 2003

Ironically, however, Fidel's father Ángel had been on the opposite side of the struggle as Martí. Ángel was a Galician conscript in the Spanish army sent to suppress Cuba's rising independent movement. During the Spanish-American War of 1898, Cuba was freed from the Spanish yoke only to come under American domination, and the Spaniard Ángel Castro chose to remain in the country as an immigrant. He eventually became a wealthy landowner and sugar producer, and beginning in the 1920's he had several children with his household servant Lina Ruz González, 25 years younger and from humble origins in Pinar del Río.

Fidel was the third of these children, and he has claimed that the illegitimate status of his birth marked him in his early years. The stigmatism started from birth, as Fidel initially went by the surname Ruz rather than Castro. He also claimed that he was teasingly called a "Jew" by his childhood playmates because he had not been baptized at birth. Fidel has alleged that this outsider status instilled in him sympathy for the marginalized and poor, but the reality is that he was brought up in relative luxury under the roof of a wealthy father. Moreover, when his parents ultimately married and had him baptized, the initial stigmas that may have afflicted him dissipated and left him as typical child of the prosperous landowning classes. At the same time, Fidel credited his father with assisting poorer classes and claimed it had an impact on him, telling an interviewer, "[Angel] was there, went out and saw people every day, he had no bodyguards or people who looked after his safety. He went alone along many kilometers, and people would approach him and had access to him. They had no access to the president of an enterprise, like United Fruit or others in New York, and that is why conditions were more humane under my father. I saw all that, and it helped a lot to mold my character."

By most accounts, including his own, Fidel was a mediocre student in his early school years and dedicated most of his passion to sports and physical activity. He was also a rebellious child with a stubborn streak, and these characteristics may have been factors in his withdrawal from local schools. He was eventually removed to Santiago, the regional capital, and placed in a prestigious, rigorous, and strict Jesuit-run academy. If that sounds like a bad fit for Fidel, it's because it was; Fidel would later quip, "When I was a young boy, my father taught me that to be a good Catholic, I had to confess at church if I ever had impure thoughts about a girl. That very evening, I had to rush to confess my sin. And the next night, and the next. After a week, I decided religion wasn't for me." In one interview last decade, however, Castro extolled the virtues of Spanish Jesuits who aligned themselves with Francisco Franco during the infamous Civil War, saying, they "combined the tradition of the Jesuits—a military spirit, their military organization—with the Spanish character. The Spanish Jesuit knows how to inculcate a great sense of personal dignity, the sense of personal honor, he knows how to appreciate character, frankness, rectitude, the person's courage, the capacity to endure sacrifice. They are values that he knows how to extol."

From Santiago, the young Fidel moved on to the national capital, Havana, where he was enrolled in an even more exclusive Jesuit school, the Colegio de Belén. From there, he followed a typical path of the country's elite class and enrolled in the University of Havana to study law in 1945. Although his enthusiasm for sport and competition had remained his dominant interest up to this point, and according to his own account he had remained steadfastly apolitical while at Belén, the atmosphere of the University of Havana was bound to change all that. Student culture at the country's major institution of higher education had become highly politicized through involvement in the political turmoil that had consumed the country since the presidency of Gerardo Machado from 1925-1933. Castro's earliest commitments were to Cuban nationalism and opposition to U.S. imperialism in the Caribbean and Latin America. Cuba's president at the time, Ramón Grau, had been a promising social reformist in his earlier career but was now regarded as deeply corrupt and compromised. Grau used violent means to suppress student dissent, and the student culture itself became violent in turn, which devolved into a kind of gang war between opposing political factions. For Castro, who had never shied away from physical combat, this was a galvanizing and radicalizing environment.

A picture of the University of Havana in the 1930s

Castro's icon and mentor in his student years was the charismatic young leader of the new Ortodoxo ("Orthodox") party, Eduardo "Eddy" Chibás. Also a native of Oriente province and a graduate of Belén, Chibás became the most compelling voice of opposition against the Grau government by the middle of the 1940s. Castro first rose to wider prominence as an outspoken supporter of Chibás' bid for the presidency of Cuba in the 1948 elections, as well as becoming a leader of the youth wing of the Ortodoxo party. Castro accumulated a great deal of political capital by positioning himself as close to Chibás as he could and presenting himself as the older leader's protégé. Whether or not their relationship was as close as it seemed remains a subject of debate. In any case, it was as an Ortodoxo leader that the young Fidel's meteoric rise as a political leader truly began, a notable fact since the Ortodoxo ideology was anti-Communist. There were a number of communist and socialist factions active in Havana at the time, but Castro's initial commitments were to nationalism, anti-imperialism, and a generic doctrine of social justice. Such were the pillars of Chibás' Ortodoxo ideology, largely derived from the ideas of José Martí, whose mantle Castro himself would later claim to assume.

Chibás

As would continue to be the case for the rest of his life, Fidel Castro's single-minded focus on Cuban autonomy did not keep him aloof from foreign affairs. To the contrary, he became embroiled in the political struggles of two other countries in the region while still a student. Castro took part in a failed attempt to overthrow Rafael Trujillo, the U.S.-backed dictator of the Dominican Republic. In concert with a force of Dominican exiles, Castro and his Cuban allies set out on a maritime expedition with about 1,200 men, but things literally did not get very far. Tipped off on the effort by U.S. and Dominican intelligence, Cuba's President Grau sent the Cuban military out to stop the mission and arrest the participants. As the story goes, Fidel escaped arrest by leaping overboard and swimming back to shore, not the last time his immense physical prowess would prove helpful to keeping his political ambitions alive.

Fidel's second important encounter with regional politics outside Cuba found him in Bogotá, Colombia for a student congress at the time of the assassination of Liberal leader Jorge Eliécer Gaitán, a proponent of nationalism and leftist social policy. Bloody riots and armed conflict followed, with Castro joining some of Gaitán's supporters in combat. Castro explained his involvement in Bogotá:

"I joined the people; I grabbed a rifle in a police station that collapsed when it was rushed by a crowd. I witnessed the spectacle of a totally spontaneous revolution...that experience led me to identify myself even more with the cause of the people. My still incipient Marxist ideas had nothing to do with our conduct – it was a spontaneous reaction on our part, as young people with Martí-an, anti-imperialist, anti-colonialist and pro-democratic ideas."

This involvement gave the 21-year old student publicity in the Havana press, increasing his political profile. Castro would also fault a lack of political organization for the failures, further cementing his opinion that a revolution could only succeed if the leaders of the revolution maintained a solid grip on as much power as possible.

Gaitán

In subsequent years, Castro remained in Havana. Chibás lost his election bid to Grau's appointed successor, Carlos Prío, a devastating disappointment to his young supporters, but there were other things on Castro's mind. Within a few days of Prío's inauguration, Fidel married Mirta Díaz Balart, a philosophy student he had met in Havana. Mirta came from a wealthy and politically influential family, also based in Oriente province, and her father paid for the couple's honeymoon to the United States, an ironic choice given the groom's strong anti-American sentiments. In fact, it was in New York City, the center of capitalist finance, that Fidel Castro purchased a copy of Karl Marx's *Das Kapital*, as well as other works by Marx, Friedrich Engels, and Vladimir Lenin. Castro discussed how he felt upon reading these extremely influential works:

"Marxism taught me what society was. I was like a blindfolded man in a forest, who doesn't even know where north or south is. If you don't eventually come to truly understand the history of the class struggle, or at least have a clear idea that society is divided between the rich and the poor, and that some people subjugate and exploit other people, you're lost in a forest, not knowing anything."

Castro astutely told an interviewer of his recognition of Lenin's problem trying to secure the Bolshevik Revolution in 1917 while also operating under the belief that "there could not be revolution in only one country and that there had to be simultaneous revolution everywhere, on the basis of the great development of the productive forces." The fact that the Soviet Union became the world's first truly Communist nation was made all the more ironic by the fact that Russia was among the most backwards and least industrialized nations in Europe at the time, conditions that Marxists assumed did not make Russia ripe for revolution.

Upon their return and his graduation from law school, Fidel practiced law and tried to support his new family, all the while remaining deeply enmeshed in politics. He moved to the left ideologically, but he remained loyal to Eddy Chibás and the Ortodoxo party. Chibás' 1951 suicide was a tragic setback, and perhaps gave further encouragement to Castro's burgeoning sense that only armed revolution could bring about genuine change in Cuba. Given Castro's forceful personality, it would not take long for events to confirm this newfound conviction.

Chapter 4: The Movement

Even given his prominence as a young supporter of Chibás, few could have predicted that 26 year old Fidel Castro would pose the first serious and violent challenge to the legitimacy of strongman Fulgencio Batista's rule, which succeeded the brief, corrupt, and largely inept regime of Carlos Prío. Batista, a military general who had already held the Cuban presidency between 1933-1944, returned to power in 1952 in a *coup d'état*, suspending the 1940 democratic constitution he himself had signed into law and assuming an array of dictatorial powers. Batista's coup was assisted by the fact that Cuba's nationalist opposition was suffering from an acute leadership vacuum after the suicide of Chibás.

Batista

Into this vacuum stepped Castro, who had planned to run as an Ortodoxo congressional candidate in the 1952 elections before they were suspended by Batista's putsch. The electoral route to the achievement of his political ambitions was now closed to him, but he was convinced that Batista's rule rested on shaky foundations, and that a concerted assault could bring it crumbling to the ground. It is not clear how familiar he was with the ideas of Vladimir Lenin at this point, but Castro's notion that a small vanguard of revolutionaries could spearhead a revolution was straight out of the 1917 Bolshevik playbook, albeit ultimately less successful in its outcome.

Along with his brother Raúl and other allies, Fidel began to stockpile weapons and organize a secret opposition movement known as "The Movement", which had both civil and military committees. The conspirators chose the Moncada barracks of Santiago, one of the country's largest military garrisons, as the target of their audacious assault on the ruling regime. The plan was to catch the garrison during a holiday, when much of its active force would be away, seizing allowing them to seize control of it and weaken the army's strategic hold on the province. In the meantime, they hoped, a popular revolt would emerge in support of their efforts. Castro's plan was extremely similar to the kind of raids conducted by Marti and his men against the Spanish generations earlier.

Although Castro was now breaking decisively with the nonviolent and political opposition methods espoused by the Ortodoxo party, he was still ideologically aligned with Chibás' movement, and most of his soldiers in the Moncada attack came from the ranks of the Ortodoxos. However, he remained at a distance from the Socialists and Communists, partly because he hoped to achieve the widest possible base of popular support and avoid alienating political moderates.

Before the attack, Castro exhorted his followers with the promise of victory in one form or another:

"In a few hours you will be victorious or defeated, but regardless of the outcome – listen well, friends – this Movement will triumph. If you win tomorrow, the aspirations of Marti will be fulfilled sooner. If we fail, our action will nevertheless set an example for the Cuban people, and from the people will arise fresh new men willing to die for Cuba. They will pick up our banner and move forward... The people will back us in Oriente and in the whole island. As in '68 and '92, here in Oriente we will give the first cry of Liberty or Death!"

In military terms, the attack on the Moncada Barracks on July 26, 1953 was a catastrophic failure, perhaps unsurprisingly for a leader with no military experience. Poorly armed and badly outnumbered, the rebels were routed, and some of them never even reached the barracks. Of Castro's approximately 160 companions, 60 were killed in the assault and dozens more were captured and tortured to death by Batista's police. Castro himself, along with his brother Raúl and a number of his closest associates, was captured, tried, and imprisoned. Naturally, Batista used the events to crack down further on his political opponents, including members of the Ortodoxo.

Nevertheless, the attack proved to be a political watershed and the true origin of Fidel Castro's successful revolutionary career, even if not in the way he initially intended. His trial in particular would provide Castro with a highly public platform from which to galvanize popular sentiment against Batista. The speech he delivered at his trial was subsequently published in a series of sold-out editions and became the manifesto for what became known as the July 26 Movement. In the speech, he declared, "I know that jail will be as hard as it has ever been for anyone, filled with threats, with vileness, and cowardly brutality; but I do not fear this, as I do not fear the fury of the miserable tyrant who snuffed out the life of seventy brothers of mine. Condemn me, it does not matter. History will absolve me!" The defiant final line of the speech echoed across the Cuban political landscape for decades.

Fidel Castro under arrest after the Moncada attack.

The time in prison tightened the bonds between the Castro brothers and their closest allies, and it allowed them to engage in collective ideological study. Raúl was already a Marxist by this point, but Castro was either not entirely convinced by Marxism yet or chose to defer his public espousal of socialist ideology for reasons of political expediency. Fidel had managed to maintain control of the Movement from jail, and 1954 saw the publication of *History Will Absolve Me*, in which he prophetically explained, "I would honestly love to revolutionize this country from one end to the other! I am sure this would bring happiness to the Cuban people. I would not be stopped by the hatred and ill will of a few thousand people, including some of my relatives, half the people I know, two-thirds of my fellow professionals, and four-fifths of my ex-schoolmates."

Raul Castro and Che Guevara

In the summer of 1955, after a resounding victory in an election widely regarded as fraudulent, Batista chose to pardon and release the 26 of July Movement leaders. The choice may seem surprising, but Batista was under pressure to avoid the appearance of dictatorship and illegitimacy. Furthermore, he was evidently quite confident after the election in the solidity of his status and regarded Castro and his allies as little more than a distraction, not a major threat. Meanwhile, during prison, Castro had divorced Mirta, whom he had repudiated for taking a job in Batista's government; she, meanwhile, was understandably frustrated with having been abandoned to raise their young son, Fidelito, alone while her husband engaged in suicidal political maneuvers. Upon his release from prison, Fidel was once again a bachelor, free to immerse himself entirely into building up the movement he had spearheaded.

Fidel did not stay long in Cuba after his release. His vocal activism was enough to give Batista second thoughts a mere month after the amnesty was signed. Anti-government violence had broken out across Havana, and although it was not clear Castro had much of a leadership role in any of it, he wrote articles and gave radio-broadcasted speeches supporting and encouraging it. Batista had resorted to extrajudicial assassinations previously, and Castro and his supporters began to fear for their lives in the climate of violence that took hold over the summer. On June 24, 1955, Raúl Castro fled Cuba for Mexico, and his older brother followed on July 7. In a final article published in the opposition magazine *Bohemia*, Fidel wrote: "I am leaving Cuba because all doors of peaceful struggle have been closed to me . . . As a follower of Martí, I believe the time has come to take rights and not to beg for them, to fight instead of pleading for them . . .

From trips such as this, one does not return or else one returns with the tyranny beheaded at one's feet."

Fidel Castro was about to put his money where his mouth was.

Chapter 5: The Cuban Revolution

"I am not a liberator. Liberators do not exist. The people liberate themselves." - Che

In the early months of 1956, supporters of Castro's Movimiento 26 de Julio began to converge in Mexico City from Cuba and various places of exile. Castro, based in Mexico since his exile began, had begun secretly planning a rebel military invasion of the island, which was to occur later that same year. Now was the time to gather his men and start preparing them to take on Batista's much larger and better-equipped army.

It would have been an insane proposition had Castro and his inner circle still not been firmly convinced despite their previous failures that the Cuban populace would ultimately rally to their side against the government. Their training involved, first and foremost, building physical stamina in anticipation of a long and grueling struggle, and making soldiers of men who for the most part lacked real military experience. This included grueling marches around Mexico City, hikes up the towering hills and volcanoes that surrounded the city, and training in self-defense techniques. As for the military preparation, a Castro supporter named Alberto Bayo took charge of imparting instruction in firearms use and marksmanship. Bayo, who had been an officer on the Republican side of the Spanish Civil War, was the member of the group most experienced in the kind of conflict that awaited the rebels in Cuba.

Bayo

It was around this time that Castro accepted a new crucial ally into his inner circle, a young Argentine doctor named Ernesto Guevara de la Serna. Known as "El Che", an affectionate term for Argentines among Latin Americans based on the frequently used Argentine slang interjection "che", Che had recently witnessed and been transformed by the CIA-sponsored coup against Guatemala's legitimately elected president, Jacobo Arbenz. That experience motivated the Marxist Che to take up the struggle against imperialism. Che treated allergy patients at Mexico City's General Hospital, gave lectures on medicine to university students, and became involved in laboratory research projects. On the political front, he extended and solidified his bonds with exiled Latin American revolutionaries, particularly the Cubans. As early as May 1955, he expressed in a letter home an enthusiasm for going to Cuba, which he viewed as ripe for revolution, but his intentions were not yet fixed: he also discussed the possibility of going to New York, Europe, or China.

By the end of 1955, Che had two potential paths before him. With his wife Hilda, who became pregnant in that year and gave birth in February 1956, he had the prospect of a comfortable settled life in Mexico, with work of the sort he had been pursuing for years. On the other hand, with Fidel Castro, he now saw the possibility of becoming part of the vanguard of a revolution that, as he saw it, would strike at the heart of U.S. power in the region. Given his previous background as a seeker of adventure, it is not really surprising which path he ultimately chose to take. Although Che and Castro had famously contrasting personalities, Che decided to join Castro's movement, perhaps because, as he later wrote, "The desire to sacrifice an entire lifetime to the noblest of ideals serves no purpose if one works alone." Che also characterized Batista as a "U.S. puppet whose strings needed cutting."

Che had originally imagined his participation in the Cuban anti-Batista struggle as being mainly medical in focus, providing essential care to the rebels during what was likely to be a brutal campaign. But he began to attend shooting range sessions with the Castro brothers and their allies, and he soon revealed himself to be a surprisingly accurate shot for someone with no martial background. Che soon impressed Bayo with his performance in all areas of training. His now apparent abilities, combined with a strong personal connection to both Fidel and Raúl, resulted in his rapid elevation to a leadership role in the group.

Castro's original plan was to make the invasion coincide with the anniversary of the July 26 Moncada assault, but circumstances got in the way. The Mexican police got wind of the group's large-scale arms and ammunition stockpiles and, under pressure from Batista's government, arrested and incarcerated a number of them. While they were ultimately set free, the raid constituted a major setback for the movement, and they did not manage to launch their invasion until near the end of November 1956.

The setbacks continued after they set off. Traveling on a rickety yacht, the legendary *Granma*, the rebels hit choppy seas while crossing the Gulf of Mexico, and most became horribly seasick. The adverse conditions resulted in a two-day delay, ruining their plans to meet with an allied clandestine rebel group in Cuba. The arrival was planned to coincide with an uprising in Santiago, Cuba's southern port, but instead the revolt began while they were still out at sea, giving Batista's army an advance warning and allowing Cuban troops to amass in and around Santiago. Shortly after arriving on December 2, Castro and his 82 companions were caught in an ambush, and most were killed or captured. Remarkably, though, the leaders of the group survived and reunited once the chaos had subsided, including the Castro brothers, Che, and a few others. They fled into the high, treacherous, and thickly forested Sierra Maestra mountain range that runs alongside Cuba's southern coast. Che would write that these days were "the most painful days of the war", and Castro would later explain how the hardships led to the growth of the beards by which the Cuban rebels became famous:

"The story of our beards is very simple: it arose out of the difficult conditions we were living and fighting under as guerrillas. We didn't have any razor blades... everybody just let their beards and hair grow, and that turned into a kind of badge of identity. For the campesinos and everybody else, for the press, for the reporters we were 'los barbudos' - the bearded ones. It had its positive side: in order for a spy to infiltrate us, he had to start preparing months ahead of time - he'd have had to have six-months' growth of beard, you see... Later, with the triumph of the Revolution, we kept our beards to preserve the symbolism."

The first stage of operations having failed miserably, the rebels moved on to the second set of tasks of the insurgency: building a network of support among the local peasantry, recruiting new fighters, and establishing connections with sympathetic groups in other parts of the country. In all of these areas they proved more successful. Already by the end of December, they had begun to train locals who wanted to join the revolutionary force. The impoverished and marginal peasantry of the Sierra Maestra had little access to education, electricity, or medical care, and the promises of equality and redistribution put forth by the rebels had an obvious resonance with many of them. Their knowledge of the countryside was an invaluable resource, as none of the invaders had much familiarity with the territory.

On the other hand, the endurance and loyalty of the new recruits was always shaky, and it was Che who began putting great effort into vetting the newcomers and trying to identify potential weaknesses before they became a liability. He became one of the most ruthless of Castro's various commanders, harsh with recruits he regarded as cowards, likely deserters, or traitors, and he was never afraid to use the ultimate punishment of execution. When a peasant army guide named Eutimio Guerra admitted he had given away the rebels' position to Batista's forces for the promise of ten thousand pesos, he knew he was facing execution and asked for a quick death. Che stepped forward and shot him in the head, describing the event in his diaries, "The situation was uncomfortable for the people and for Eutimio, so I ended the problem giving him a shot with a .32 pistol in the right side of the brain...He gasped for a little while and was dead. Upon proceeding to remove his belongings I couldn't get off the watch tied by a chain to his belt, and then he told me in a steady voice farther away than fear: 'Yank it off, boy, what does it matter.' I did so and his possessions were now mine." Che's ferocity and asceticism seems to have impressed Castro deeply, and it influenced both of their increasingly ambitious goals for post-revolutionary social transformation.

From their inauspicious beginnings, the rebels did gradually expand their operations through recruitment, alliance, and growing support from the populace. A pivotal moment came in March 1957, when an affiliated group of urban guerrillas attempted to storm the Presidential Palace and assassinate Batista. The effort ended in failure, but it also seemed to signal the weakness and vulnerability of the regime, and it galvanized opposition among the public, which largely sympathized with the would-be assassins. The situation was exacerbated by the increasing brutality Batista unleashed against anyone suspected of involvement in subversive activity. Batista's illegitimacy and weakness was confirmed when the United States withdrew support from his government and imposed sanctions to express disapproval of the chaos and violence that now consumed Cuba. Through the same period, the guerrillas took all measures they could to consolidate their legitimacy in the eyes of Cubans and the international community. On the latter front, they were helped when *New York Times* journalist Herbert Matthews sought them out in February 1957. Matthews published an extensive and sympathetic interview with Castro, which placed him in the eyes of the world as an idealistic, authoritative, and morally serious freedom fighter who, Matthews assured his readers, had no truck with communism. It is true that, for the moment, Castro had no declared allegiance to Marxist doctrines, although Raul and

Che were not the only members of his inner circle who did. His goal was to assemble as wide a coalition as possible to achieve the overthrow of Batista and sort out ideological differences later.

By early 1958, the rebels had successfully beaten back a number of relatively small incursions by Batista's forces, who were nevertheless always more numerous than their opponents. Castro noted that his Comandante, Che, "had great moral authority over his troops", but that Che took so many risks Castro felt he had a "tendency toward foolhardiness". Che's bravery in battle also won him the admiration of his men, and one of his lieutenants, Joel Iglesias, wrote that upon his being wounded, "Che ran out to me, defying the bullets, threw me over his shoulder, and got me out of there. The guards didn't dare fire at him ... later they told me he made a great impression on them when they saw him run out with his pistol stuck in his belt, ignoring the danger, they didn't dare shoot."

Che in Las Villas province, Cuba, November 1958.

Batista appointed General Eulogio Cantillo to be in charge of the large-scale offensive, "Operación Verano," and gave him more than half of the Cuban regular army, amounting to a force of about 12,000. Given that the rebels still only numbered a few hundred, the sides were as disproportionate as could be. On the other hand, Cantillo's army entered the area with some weaknesses. Having been in the Sierra Maestra for over a year, Castro, Che, and the rest of the revolutionaries knew the territory far better than the invaders, and they had also developed a support network among the local populace. Moreover, almost all of them had now experienced some combat due to regular conflict with small army patrols and local government supporters, while more than half of the men sent out with the army were poorly trained new recruits with no experience and a basic lack of support for the government's cause.

As it turned out, the offensive would be the most disastrous move Batista could make. In a series of skirmishes, the Cuban army was repeatedly outfoxed by the revolutionaries. They repeatedly led army battalions into ambushes and then managed to scatter back into the surrounding wilderness. Repeatedly, the consequence was a disproportionate casualty ratio: in their first several clashes with Cantillo's army, the rebels lost fewer than ten men in total, while army casualties soon exceeded 100. The first major battle of the offensive took place at the mouth of the La Plata River, beginning on July 11, 1958. Although the confrontation began with a successful attempt to lead Castro into a trap, the army systematically showed its weakness and poor morale, resulting in hundreds of troops surrendering. The rebels handed their captives over to the Red Cross, although a few, including the commanding officer of the defeated battalion, defected to the other side.

The humiliating setback at La Plata was the beginning of the end for the army, although the air force managed to do some damage to rebel positions with constant bombardments, and Cantillo showed a flash of tactical brilliance on July 29. At the village of Las Mercedes, he dispatched a line of troops near a position held by Castro, attempting to solicit an ambush. The ploy succeeded, and the handful of rebels now found themselves ambushed by a much larger army force that had not been visible from their previous position. It was Che who determined that Cantillo had dispatched his troops in a triangular formation, with the intention of gradually surrounding the rebels; with a small command, Che successfully intercepted a group of approaching army reinforcements and took 50 soldiers captive. The battle had now reached a standstill between the two sides, and Castro sent a message to Cantillo requesting the opening of negotiations. Surprisingly, given that the army's numbers were still far superior and the rebels were now in the weakest position they had occupied since the start of the offensive, Cantillo consulted with Batista and finally agreed to open negotiations. After a series of stalling tactics on both sides, and uncertain negotiations with an emissary of Batista's, the offensive came to an end quietly: both sides used the cover of the ceasefire to withdraw. The battle over the Sierra Maestra was now over.

Although they had proven unable to defeat Cantillo's army militarily, Castro, Che, and the other rebels had conclusively demonstrated the weakness of Batista's ostensibly far superior forces. It was now time to take the battle closer to Havana, the capital and center of Batista's power base. Fidel's brother Raúl had already begun operations in the eastern Oriente province, missing out on the Operación Verano conflict while building a large and disciplined force. It was decided that Fidel and Raúl would remain in the southeast and focus on consolidating their strength and taking the city of Santiago, while Che and his fellow commander Camilo Cienfuegos would strike out to the West, toward Havana.

They proceeded on foot, descending from the mountains of the Sierra Maestra into the flatlands or *llano* that lay to the West. The rainy season had arrived, and the land was swampy and cut up by numerous swollen rivers. Aerial patrols dogged them by day, so they took to traveling mainly in the dark to avoid their deadly attacks. Despite the adverse conditions, Che and Camilo were highly successful in their campaign, capturing town after town for the rebels and fighting off army incursions over four months. The crowning achievement of the offensive was the capture of the city of Santa Clara on December 31, where they also seized control of a supply train containing large quantities of weapons and ammunition. What had begun as a tiny isolated movement now looked like an unstoppable tide. Simultaneously with the capture of Santa Clara, the Castro brothers took control of the prominent city of Santiago. The eastern half of Cuba was now essentially under rebel control.

As it turned out, Batista was not one to hold on doggedly to power. On the night of December 31, 1958, he fled the country with his closest allies and a large sum of cash and headed to the Dominican Republic. Upon leaving, he named Judge Carlos Manuel Piedra as president and Cantillo as head of the armed forces, but few in Cuba were paying attention to these developments: all were awaiting the next move of the *barbudos*, the bearded rebels whose exploits had now captured the imagination of the country. Upon hearing the news of the dictator's departure, Che Guevara and Camilo Cienfuegos set out for Havana, where they arrived on January 2. Fidel Castro had orders for them: each was to take over one of the major military garrisons of the city. Fidel had already made a series of decisions about the initial transition of power, all of which suggested a cautious desire to establish a distance from the more radical politics espoused by Che and Raúl, among others. Discarding Batista's last-ditch appointments, he selected his own transitional president and prime minister: the moderate Manuel Urrutia, a liberal lawyer with international connections, and José Miró. Fidel reserved the position of commander in chief of the armed forces for himself. The Marxists were initially given less public roles, as their vocal beliefs had already become a major source of suspicion for the United States at a point when Fidel still hoped for friendly relations with Cuba's biggest neighbor.

Fidel received a public hero's welcome when he arrived in the capital on January 8, 1959, and he initially tried to use his folk hero status to work as a unifying force, staying aloof from the initial wranglings of the provisional government. Che performed an important and controversial function in the early months after the fall of Batista: purging the ranks of the Cuban army of Batista loyalists, war criminals, and informants. He had been ruthless against deserters, informants, and cowards during the guerrilla campaign, and Castro clearly trusted him not to shy away from what was to be an unpleasant task. The exact number of executions carried out under his orders remains controversial, with a lower estimate of 55 and higher estimates adding about 100 more to the tally. Either way, such executions were fully justified as well as essential in Che's eyes. Arbenz's government had fallen in Guatemala, he believed, in part because the army remained full of disloyal officers who ultimately took part in the coup. In the meantime, he composed and delivered a speech proposing his version of agrarian reform, with members of the Partido Socialista Popular as his audience; he also began the composition of his book Guerrilla Warfare, which used his two years of martial experience as the basis for an instructional study of insurgent combat methods. On the personal front, he announced to Hilda, who arrived in late

January, that he was now in love with another woman, Aleida March, and Hilda accepted a divorce.

Aleida with Castro and Che

Che was declared a Cuban citizen "by birth" on February 9, by way of a new clause in the revised Constitution that conferred citizenship on foreigners who had fought against Batista. By then, however, Castro was mired in implacable conflict with the transitional leadership he had helped appoint, and he now essentially insisted that they defer to his authority on controversial matters. Miró, the prime minister, resigned in protest of the commander-in-chief's coercive approach, and Fidel then took the position for himself. Now in a more central and visible role, he began to steer things more clearly in a radical direction. However, he remained initially solicitous of the colossus to the north, hoping to avoid an enmity that was already looming as inevitable once Castro systematically alienated the moderates and liberals who had not long before been his allies. He toured the United States in April, where Herbert Mathews' *New York Times* articles had made him a sympathetic figure for many, but the visiting Cuban revolutionary was treated coldly by the Eisenhower administration, and he came out of his meeting with Vice President Richard Nixon far less hopeful about the possibility of friendly relations.

In June 1959, Castro sent Che on a several-month diplomatic tour of the Middle East and Asia. Most of the countries were recently independent, former colonial nations that had joined together at the 1955 Bandung Conference to advocate economic autonomy, development, and cooperation. Che's mission was to convey goodwill and kindred spirit of the new Cuban regime, negotiate favorable trade relations with as many of the countries as possible, and see what he could learn from their experiences of decolonization and reform. The trip would initiate one of Che's major initiatives of the subsequent decade: the creation of a unified "Tricontinental" of developing and formerly colonial countries adequate to stand up to the imperialist meddling of the United States and other powerful industrialized countries.

By the summer 1959, the mood in Cuba was highly confrontational, in part because of the passage and implementation of an agricultural reform bill promulgated by Fidel Castro under the influence of the more radical ideas of Raúl and Che. Landowners began to protest the seizure and redistribution of the land, and the more moderate supporters of the revolution now suspected Castro to have communist sympathies. The nationalization of foreign-owned companies and assets by the government strengthened these suspicions, and increased United States hostility to the new government. But Castro and his allies hunkered down, with Castro himself becoming head of the newly formed Instituto Nacional de Reforma Agraria (INRA), charged with implementing the new land reforms. Even more alarmingly to moderates, Castro named Che head of Cuba's National Bank and Minister of Finance. Since Che's only known background in economics was his reading of Marx's *Das Kapital*, it became clear that Castro's intention was to radically reorient the economy around central planning and redistribution of property. Urrutia, still hanging on as President, denounced the increasing communist influence on policy, and in the confrontation that followed, he was forced to resign. As Che himself noted, "When asked whether or not we are Marxists, our position is the same as that of a physicist or a biologist when asked if he is a 'Newtonian,' or if he is a 'Pasteurian.' There are truths so evident, so much a part of people's knowledge, that it is now useless to discuss them."

Once Castro felt emboldened enough to embrace socialism, he trumpeted it:

"I became a Communist on my own, before reading a book by Marx, Engels, Lenin, or anyone. I became a Communist by studying capitalist political economy, and when I had some understanding of that problem, it ac-tually seemed to me so absurd, so irrational, so inhuman, that I simply began to elaborate on my own formulas for production and distribution. That was when I was a third-year law student at the University of Ha-vana. And I'll tell you something more, because I do not hide my life, nor my origin, nor do I have any reason to invent things. If I were a false man, if my ideas were not deep and sincere, I would not have been able to convince anyone in this country, because when the revolution triumphed, the majority of the people were not Socialists, and the majority of the people were not Communists. But when the revolution triumphed, my convictions were Socialist, were Communist. I was born within a landholding family, I studied in religious schools, that is, my primary and secondary education. I arrived at the University of Havana being a political illiterate and no one instilled ideas in me. These ideas were the result of my own analysis and my own meditations. I am very sorry not to have had, since I was a child, someone who would have educated me politically. Since I had to discover that on my own, I became what could be called a utopian Communist. Then I discovered Marxist literature, the Communist Manifesto, the works of Marx, Engels, and Lenin. Maybe there are some in Cuba and even outside of Cuba who remember listen-ing to all the criticisms that I made about capitalist society when I had not even read one Marxist document ... Before the revolution, our program was not yet a Socialist program ... It was a program of national liberation, very close to socialism. I would say that it was the maximum that at that time and under those circumstances could have been understood by the masses of the population. Although our program was not Socialist as of yet, I did myself have deep Socialist and Communist convictions. When the revolution triumphed, the people were still not Socialists or Communists because they were still too deceived, too poisoned through anti-Communist propaganda, McCarthyist propaganda, too poisoned by bourgeois papers, bourgeois books, bourgeois cinema coming exclusively from the United States ... What made our people Socialists and Communists? The revolutionary laws, the work of the revolution, persuasion, and education ... Now the people are Socialists and Communists ... That is a reality, and it is not going to change, no matter how many millions of tourists come here."

With Che now de facto head of the Cuban economy, he and Fidel began to propose its reorganization along lines even more radical than the communist economies of the Eastern Bloc had attempted: they wished to replace wage labor altogether with an ethic of work driven entirely by "moral incentives," in which all commitment to individual advancement and personal wealth would disappear in favor of a devotion to collective social well-being. True socialism, Che contended, relied on the emergence of a "New Man" who no longer exhibited the selfishness of capitalist society. In the face of such hostile rhetoric, Cuba's wealth began to flow out of the country along with a large part of the upper and middle class. With the United States and its European allies now hardened in their hostility to the new government, under Castro's direction, Cuba signed a comprehensive trade pact with the Soviet Union in February 1960.

The battle lines were now drawn, placing Cuban-U.S. relations within the Cold War dichotomy that had first divided Europe in the wake of World War II and then spread across Asia during Mao's rise in China, the Korean War, and the struggle for independence in Indochina.

Fidel and Che marching in Havana, 1960

Chapter 6: Cuba and the Cold War

"We are not executing innocent people or political opponents. We are executing murderers, and they deserve it." – Fidel Castro, 1959.

During the early 1960s, as the relationship between Cuba and the United States was growing implacably confrontational, Castro was also in the process of radically restructuring Cuba's economy and society. Because the Soviet Union had become Cuba's protector and sponsor against U.S. aggression, Soviet socialism became the predominant model not only for economic reorganization but for the various forms of political suppression that Castro undertook during the early years of his leadership. In response to questions about why Cuba had no reelections, Castro stated in 1961, "The revolution has no time for elections. There is no more democratic government in Latin America than the revolutionary government...If Mr. Kennedy does not like Socialism, we do not like imperialism. We do not like capitalism."

The 26 of July Movement and several allied, socialist-leaning groups were consolidated into a single party, and other political organizations were effectively banned from public life. Also subject to persecution were homosexuals and others labeled "deviants" in the new austere code of communist rule. Castro oversaw the creation of an official state press organ, *Granma*, which essentially expressed the new "party line" on current events and issues.

Two further events would ensure that Castro's Cuba and the United States became implacable enemies. The first was the April 1961 Bay of Pigs invasion. Within just a month of becoming President, the issue of communist Cuba became central to the Kennedy Presidency. On February 3rd, 1961, President Kennedy called for a plan to support Cuban refugees in the U.S. A month later, Kennedy created the Peace Corps, a program that trained young American volunteers to help with economic and community development in poor countries. Both programs were integral pieces of the Cold War: each was an attempt to align disadvantaged groups abroad with the United State and the West, against the Soviet Union and its Communist satellites.

Castro railed against CIA involvement among Cubans trying to overthrow Castro and the still young revolution. In March 1961, Castro spoke in Havana and told Cubans:

Openly and unabashedly they are organizing training camps; openly and unabashedly they are building air bases and air strips. Everyone knows who is building the strips and buying planes, that mercenaries are recruiting troops. They even have the cynicism to publish photographs.

Cuba is not located in Africa or on the planet Mars; Cuba is in this hemisphere. Our air space is being violated constantly by planes which do not come from Venus, Africa, or the South Pole, but from this continent. As proof we need only remember that while there is talk of security, our country is kept under constant watch by planes based on this continent, from the United States to Guatemala. Without respect for international law, not only are they openly recruiting weapons but they constantly violate our air space, our jurisdictional waters. With planes and ships they bring explosives here which cost the lives of children, women, and workers, cruelly killed with no other goal than to soften our people. That is the word they use.

With terrorism and bombs they have killed women and children, they have cowardly attacked workers when they leave work, thus they are trying to create counterrevolutionary bands.

What is really offensive to our country and a flagrant violation of international law is that all these activities are directly manipulated and directed from the United States by Central Intelligence Agency agents. That is to say, from there are manipulated the strings of all the conspiracies which kill children and workers, and which cruelly and inhumanely blind lives. It is truly painful that the puppets who are playing into their hands are unaware of the strategy of the Central Intelligence Agency."

Cuba and the Cold War boiled over in April, when the Kennedy Administration moved beyond soft measures to direct action. From April 17-20, 1,400 CIA-trained Cuban exiles landed on the beaches of Western Cuba in an attempt to overthrow Fidel Castro. This plan, known as the "Bay of Pigs," had been originally drafted by the Eisenhower Administration. The exiles landed in

Cuba and were expected to be greeted by anti-Castro forces within the country. After this, the U.S. was to provide air reinforcement to the rebels, and the Castro regime would slowly be overthrown.

By April 19th, however, it became increasingly clear to Kennedy that the invasion would not work. The exiles were not, as expected, greeted by anti-Castro forces. Instead, the Cuban government captured or killed all of the invaders. No U.S. air reinforcement was ever provided, flummoxing both the exiles and American military commanders. The Bay of Pigs was an unmitigated disaster.

On April 21st, in a White House press conference, President Kennedy accepted full responsibility for the failure, which had irreparably damaged Cuban-American relations. From then on, Fidel Castro remained wary of a U.S. invasion, which would have serious implications when the USSR began planning to move missiles into Cuba, precipitating another crisis a year and a half later. Between April and the following year, the U.S. and Cuba negotiated the release of the imprisoned exiles, who were finally released in December of 1962, in exchange for $55.5 million dollars worth of food and medicine. The aborted invasion now became a nationalistic rallying cry, and it probably consolidated public support in favor of the revolutionary government.

The second, and even more severe, crisis occurred in the wake of the Bay of Pigs. Cuban and Soviet officials had begun to discuss positioning Soviet nuclear warheads in Cuba, in the "backyard" of the capitalist enemy, which had many of its own missiles positioned in the territory of NATO allies well within reach of Soviet territory.

Still questioning Kennedy's resolve, and attempting to placate the concerns of Fidel Castro following the Bay of Pigs invasion, Soviet premier Nikita Khrushchev attempted to place medium range nuclear missiles in Cuba, just 90 miles off the coast of the United States. Though Castro warned him that the act would be seen by the Americans to be aggressive, Khrushchev insisted on moving the missiles in quietly under the cover of darkness. They would serve not only as a deterrent against any invasion of Cuba but also as the ultimate first-strike capability in the event of a nuclear war.

In October 1962, with the help of spy planes, U.S. intelligence discovered the Soviets were building nuclear missile sites in Cuba. The president officially learned of this on October 16th. It went without saying that nuclear missile sites located just miles off the coast of the American mainland posed a grave threat to the country, especially because missiles launched from Cuba would reach their targets in mere minutes. That would throw off important military balances in nuclear arms and locations that had previously (and subsequently) ensured the Cold War stayed cold. Almost all senior American political figures agreed that the sites were offensive and needed to be removed, but how? Members of the U.S. Air Force wanted to take out the sites with bombing missions and launch a full-scale invasion of Cuba, but Kennedy, however, was afraid that such an action could ignite a full-scale escalation leading to nuclear war.

Kennedy's brother, Attorney General Bobby Kennedy, served as a critical advisor to the President and a counterweight to the aggressive posturing of military brass. Though he had previously taken aggressive stances in Cuba, Bobby was one of the voices who opposed outright war and helped craft the eventual plan: a blockade of Cuba. That was the decision President Kennedy ultimately reached as well, deciding on a naval blockade of all Soviet ships to be the better option.

On October 22, 1962, President Kennedy addressed the nation to inform them of the crisis. He told Americans that the "purpose of these bases can be none other than to provide a nuclear strike capability against the Western Hemisphere." Speaking of the threat to the nuclear weapon balance maintained in previous years, Kennedy stated, "For many years, both the Soviet Union and the United States, recognizing this fact, have deployed strategic nuclear weapons with great care, never upsetting the precarious status quo which insured that these weapons would not be used in the absence of some vital challenge." Thus, Kennedy announced a blockade, warning, "To halt this offensive buildup a strict quarantine on all offensive military equipment under shipment to Cuba is being initiated. All ships of any kind bound for Cuba from whatever nation or port will, if found to contain cargoes of offensive weapons, be turned back."

Kennedy speaking to the country about the Cuban Missile Crisis

Beginning on October 24th, the U.S. began inspecting all Soviet ships traveling in the Caribbean. Any ships carrying missile parts would not be allowed to enter Cuba. Additionally,

President Kennedy demanded that the Soviets remove all nuclear missile sites from Cuba. In response, Soviet premier Khrushchev called the blockade "an act of aggression propelling humankind into the abyss of a world nuclear-missile war". Castro claimed the blockade was "not only an outrage to the principle of commercial freedom, but also a flagrant violation of the U.N. Charter. It is an act of war in time of peace. But Cuba is not alone. We have friends and we are counting on international solidarity."

With the announcement of the embargo, and possibly fearing another American invasion of Cuba, Khrushchev ordered that his soldiers there could use any weapons at their disposal, as long they were not nuclear weapons. For the next four days, President Kennedy and Khrushchev were engaged in intense diplomacy that left both sides on the brink. Europeans and Americans braced for potential war, wondering whether any day might be their last. During that time, however, the Soviets used back-channel communications through Bobby Kennedy seeking a way for both sides to reach an agreement and save face. With his intimate knowledge of the situation, Bobby personally helped the President draft the plan for negotiations with the Soviets, which included removing American missiles from Turkey in exchange for the removal of Soviet missiles from Cuba. President Kennedy had created a committee, the Executive Committee (ExComm), and Attorney General Kennedy was placed on that Committee, giving Bobby enormous influence over the President's decision during the defining moment of his Presidency.

Though the Americans were unaware of it, Khrushchev had already decided to ultimately back down and remove the nuclear missiles by October 25. Finally, on October 28th, Khrushchev and President Kennedy agreed to the removal of the missiles, under U.N. supervision. In exchange, the U.S. vowed never to invade Cuba, while privately agreeing to remove intercontinental ballistic missiles (ICBMs) that had been stationed in Turkey, near the Soviet border, under the Eisenhower Administration. Realizing how close they had come to disaster, the Americans and Soviets agreed to establish a direct communication line, known as the "Hotline", between the two sides in an effort to avoid nuclear catastrophe resulting from miscommunication.

For his part, Fidel felt slighted and used at the end of the episode, since none of Cuba's outstanding grievances against the U.S. had been addressed. As the Soviets and Americans were secretly reaching an agreement to resolve the crisis, Castro told reporters, "Cuba did not and does not intend to be in the middle of a conflict between the East and the West. Our problem is above all one of national sovereignty. Cuba did not mean to get involved in the cold war."

In the meantime, Che's regime of "moral incentives" had not proven successful, and his economic program had become a source of conflict with Castro, who now wished to pursue a more practical set of policies. Che's disillusionment with the U.S.S.R. in the wake of the missile crisis, along with the perceived failure of his economic policies, led him to relinquish much of the power he had amassed in Cuba's new government, and to embark on the final stage of his career – which would turn out to be both a return to his early life of wandering, and an attempt to repeat the remarkable successes of the guerrilla campaign.

Chapter 7: Che the Global Revolutionary

"Why does the guerrilla fighter fight? We must come to the inevitable conclusion that the guerrilla fighter is a social reformer, that he takes up arms responding to the angry protest of the people against their oppressors, and that he fights in order to change the social system that keeps all his unarmed brothers in ignominy and misery." – Che, *Guerrilla Warfare*

Che undertook further diplomatic trips, but his real goals were now elsewhere: he reasoned that no revolution could succeed in one small and beleaguered country like Cuba as long as it was surrounded by a sea of hostile countries. Revolution had to be spread across the globe, and many of the poor and downtrodden countries of the Southern Hemisphere were ripe for a transformation like Cuba's. The Soviet Bloc was of no help, he now concluded, because he believed it treated the poorer countries allied with it practically no less exploitatively than the United States.

Although Che was headed in a new direction now that Castro was firmly entrenched in Cuba, he still traveled as part of the Cuban delegation to the United Nations in 1964, where he delivered a blistering speech that December in New York. Che repeated his criticisms of America and expressed solidarity with other Latin American nations as well as other regions under the sway of neo-imperialism. "Those who kill their own children and discriminate daily against them because of the color of their skin; those who let the murderers of blacks remain free, protecting them, and furthermore punishing the black population because they demand their legitimate rights as free men — how can those who do this consider themselves guardians of freedom? The government of the United States is not the champion of freedom, but rather the perpetrator of exploitation and oppression against the peoples of the world and against a large part of its own population."

Che also showed his interest in the conditions in Africa, stating in the same speech, "The final hour of colonialism has struck, and millions of inhabitants of Africa, Asia and Latin America rise to meet a new life and demand their unrestricted right to self-determination." He also railed against South Africa, "We speak out to put the world on guard against what is happening in South Africa. The brutal policy of apartheid is applied before the eyes of the nations of the world. The peoples of Africa are compelled to endure the fact that on the African continent the superiority of one race over another remains official policy, and that in the name of this racial superiority murder is committed with impunity. Can the United Nations do nothing to stop this?" During his time in New York, Che also appeared on the CBS Sunday news program Face the Nation and met a number of influential Americans, including U.S. Senator Eugene McCarthy and associates of Malcolm X. X would later describe Che as "one of the most revolutionary men in this country right now."

After his performance in New York, Che crossed the Atlantic and took a three month global tour that had him celebrating St. Patrick's Day and playing up his Irish roots in Ireland, as well as visits to China, North Korea, the United Arab Republic, Egypt, Algeria, Ghana, Guinea, Mali, Dahomey, Congo-Brazzaville and Tanzania. During the trip, Che wrote a letter to an editor in Uruguay explaining his purpose: "The laws of capitalism, blind and invisible to the majority, act upon the individual without his thinking about it. He sees only the vastness of a seemingly infinite horizon before him. That is how it is painted by capitalist propagandists, who purport to draw a lesson from the example of Rockefeller—whether or not it is true—about the possibilities of success. The amount of poverty and suffering required for the emergence of a Rockefeller, and the amount of depravity that the accumulation of a fortune of such magnitude entails, are left out of the picture, and it is not always possible to make the people in general see this." Che asserted that a revolutionary should "strive every day so that this love of living humanity will be transformed into acts that serve as examples."

When he reached Africa, Che strongly denounced the Soviet Union, culminating at a summit in Algiers in February 1965 where he proposed that the Soviet Union needed to completely restructure its economic policies. While everyone else saw the Cold War as a battle between the East and West, Che felt that the world was actually divided by the Northern hemisphere and Southern hemisphere, with the Soviets and Americans in the North oppressing the people in the South. Of course, that ideology ran counter to Castro in Cuba, who still relied heavily on the Soviets to help prop him up. When Che returned to Cuba, the now firmly Soviet-aligned Castro and his closest allies were displeased and granted Che's request to leave Cuba and foment revolution elsewhere. Che relinquished both his Cuban citizenship and his official status in the Cuban military and government in order to relieve Castro of responsibility for his forthcoming adventures, which were designed precisely to shake up the global military, economic, and political order.

Castro did, on the other hand, give his old comrade-in-arms assistance in his first endeavor: an expedition to the eastern Congo to assist a group of Marxist rebels. By private arrangement, Fidel deployed 125 Cuban troops, many veterans of the guerrilla war, to accompany Che on the risky mission. It had been difficult to decide on his first destination, and it seems like a very odd one for a Latin American revolutionary, but the ultimate choice was based on several criteria. Decolonization had left a power vacuum in Africa, and in general the United States had far less capacity to intervene in events there than in Latin America and the Western hemisphere. Thus, for Che this represented an opportunity: the building of a tri-continental coalition of colonized nations he envisioned had to start somewhere, and Africa seemed to be the place where current power structures were the least entrenched. The Congo represented a particularly vivid instance of this situation: the country had been consumed by factional conflict since its decolonization by Belgium in 1960, and the place was ripe, as Che saw it, for a united Marxist and anti-imperialist front to come in and seize the mantle of legitimacy. Since the country was located in the center of the continent, as he saw it, the pan-African revolution could radiate outward from there, in a larger-scale version of what had happened in the Sierra Maestra. By disappearing from the public stage, Che's whereabouts became a great source of intrigue, and rumors surrounding what happened to him began to circulate. Castro would respond by stating that Che would make his presence known when he decided to do so.

Che in the Congo

Ultimately, the results of Che's campaign in the Congo were disastrous. While the situation might have looked superficially the same as that of Cuba, it turned out to be a world unrecognizable to Che in most respects. He was frustrated by the factionalism and in-fighting of his supposed allies, the fragile loyalties of supporters, and the apparent corruption of a number of leadership figures among the African guerrilla fighters. He fell ill with dysentery, and his asthma returned with a vengeance in the sultry, humid air of the African jungle. Meanwhile, they were being dogged by mercenaries supporting the other side, including some anti-Castro Cubans affiliated with the C.I.A. After six of his Cuban men fell in combat and more were wounded, he decided to send them back and made arrangements for his own departure. Explaining the debacle in the Congo, Che asserted, "The human element failed. There is no will to fight. The leaders are corrupt. In a word... there was nothing to do." When he organized his diary for his time in the Congo, he wrote as a preface, "This is the history of a failure."

Che could not return publicly to Cuba, having declared that he would be fomenting revolution elsewhere, so he obtained false papers and lived an itinerant life in hiding in a number of countries, contemplating his next move. Finally, he returned to Cuba in secrecy, visiting Fidel as well as his wife and daughter and making arrangements for logistical support on the next stage of the struggle.

Che's errors in the Congo had been numerous: he had done insufficient research on the territory and culture, he had failed to test the loyalty and reliability of his ostensible comrades there, and he had failed to analyze whether the goals pursued were realistic. Evidently entranced by his own aura of strategic genius as well as his firmly entrenched ideology of global revolution, Che would make the same mistakes in his new campaign, which was driven by similar intentions to those that had motivated the Congo expedition. It would also take Che back to a land he had traveled through extensively about 15 years earlier.

Although Che had for some time considered returning to his home country of Argentina to spur action, he ended up settling on Bolivia for a number of reasons. Like Cuba in the 1950s, it was a largely peasant and agrarian society in which the rural population was assumed to be disaffected and hostile to the current governing regime. Furthermore, the Bolivian army was believed to be poorly trained and equipped and therefore highly vulnerable to the kind of large-scale surrender and desertion that had aided the Cuban rebels. Finally, as with the Congo, its location near the center of the continent made it an ideal place from which to launch a continental revolution. Guevara's theory of *focos* proposed that all revolutions, like Cuba's, radiate out from a small and well-located center of subversive activity, ultimately gaining momentum, linking up with other *focos*, and finally becoming an irresistible wave. Bolivia's own situation was of less concern than its ideal position as a launching pad for revolutions that would spill over into the larger and more strategically crucial neighboring countries. Indeed, Che stated, quite callously, to several of his companions that "Bolivia will sacrifice itself so that the conditions [for revolution] can be created in neighboring countries. We have to make Latin America another Vietnam, with its center in America."

Perpetually thinking in the grandiose terms of global revolution and the obliteration of U.S. power, Che had failed to place sufficient attention on the local conditions on the ground in Bolivia. Che evidently had little sense of the current political situation there: in apparently blithely assuming that President René Barrientos was a corrupt and brutal Batista type, he failed to observe that Bolivia's current head of state assumed the mantle of reform and was therefore relatively popular with the country's poor rural population. Moreover, he failed to assess the reliability of his own allies on the ground and received little help from Bolivia's Communist Party, which in more traditional Marxist manner saw the urban centers rather than the rural margins as the real revolutionary heartland and therefore had little sympathy for Che's strategy. Finally, he underestimated the Bolivian army, as well as the amount of support it was receiving from his great nemesis, the United States, which soon became aware of Che's presence in the country and was only too glad to see him in such a vulnerable position. As Daniel James observed of Che and Fidel, "it did not matter too much to them whether Bolivia itself was ripe for revolution or not, since the country was to serve essentially as the staging area of continental revolution." Though the strategies were imported from the Cuban experience, the approach could not have been more different, and this difference proved fatal.

Che in Bolivia, 1967

Che arrived in Bolivia on November 3, 1966, under a false name and heavy disguise, and he managed to pass through La Paz unrecognized and head for the remote southeastern region of Ñancahuazú, where one of his allies had purchased land on which his band of revolutionaries could gather and train for the coming conflict. He assembled only four men initially, all handpicked veterans of the Sierra Maestra, but Bolivian supporters, along with a few other international allies, began to trickle in over the following months.

By late March 1967, Che determined that they were ready for combat, and they ambushed a small Bolivian army unit, capturing a large quantity of weapons and ammunition. They scored several more small victories against the Bolivian military toward the middle of the year, but as the government became aware of Che's involvement and of the Cuban government's covert support for the endeavor, they stepped up aggressive pursuit of the guerrillas, taking advantage of the logistical support now offered by the C.I.A. The local population, meanwhile, never sided with the rebels and lent a good deal of support to the army. By September, the government had recouped its losses and scored several decisive victories over a now-dwindling rebel force, which it had cornered into a relatively small swath of territory.

On October 8, his forces diminished and his prospects for spreading revolution nearly hopeless, Che was wounded in a skirmish with a small Bolivian army company, which had been informed of the guerrilla group's presence by a local peasant informer. He taken into custody and, once he had been recognized, kept alive until the higher authorities could be consulted for instructions. According to Bolivian Sergeant Bernardino Huanca, the wounded Che had yelled out, "Do not shoot! I am Che Guevara and worth more to you alive than dead."

Che was tied up and brought to a mud-walled country schoolhouse in the village of La Higuera that night. That night, Che refused attempts to be interrogated, but he was polite to Bolivian soldiers, one of whom described him as looking "dreadful". According to that soldier, helicopter pilot, Jaime Nino de Guzman, Che had been shot through the right calf, his hair was full of dirt, and he was wearing rough leather sheaths for shoes. The following morning, Che asked to meet the village's schoolteacher, a 22 year old woman named Julia Cortez. Che wanted to tell Cortez that the conditions of the school were too deplorable to learn in, but Cortez had trouble looking him in the eye because his "gaze was unbearable, piercing, and so tranquil."

An army colonel and a C.I.A. agent arrived later in the day to the small mud-walled country schoolhouse where the guerrilla leader was being held. Orders for execution had apparently arrived from President Barrientos himself, and although the U.S. wished to interrogate the country's most outspoken nemesis further, C.I.A. agent Félix Rodríguez let the order be carried out. Mario Terán requested the honor of executing Che because three of his friends had been killed in the conflict against Che and his guerrillas. Some accounts claim the executioner had been selected by choosing lots.

As he was facing execution, a Bolivian soldier asked Che if he was thinking about his own immortality, to which Che replied, "No. I'm thinking about the immortality of the revolution." When Terán entered the hut, Che spoke out, "I know you've come to kill me. Shoot, coward! You are only going to kill a man!" Perhaps surprised, or simply half drunk, Terán initially hesitated before firing his semiautomatic rifle and hitting Che in the arms and legs. Not wounded fatally, Che writhed on the ground biting his wrists, possibly to avoid crying out in pain. Terán then fired several more rounds into Che, including shots to the chest and throat. Around 1:10 p.m. on October 9, 1967, the world's most famous revolutionary was dead.

In all, Che was shot nine times because the execution was carried out so as to appear that Che had perished in combat, and when the Bolivian government announced his death, they claimed that he had died in battle. To provide proof of this spectacular coup, they allowed a number of photographs of the revolutionary's emaciated, pallid cadaver to be taken and disseminated before the body was spirited away and hidden in a secret location. The location of Che's remains was finally revealed in 1997, and by special arrangements his remains were then disinterred and taken to Cuba.

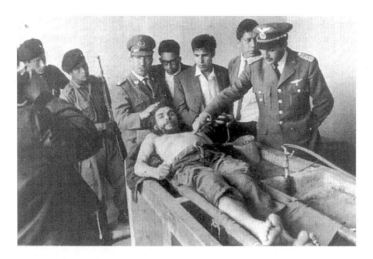

Bolivian officials gathered around Che's body

Acknowledging Che's death nearly a week later, Fidel Castro delivered a eulogy of sorts, saying of Che, "If we wish to express what we want the men of future generations to be, we must say: Let them be like Che! If we wish to say how we want our children to be educated, we must say without hesitation: We want them to be educated in Che's spirit! If we want the model of a man, who does not belong to our times but to the future, I say from the depths of my heart that such a model, without a single stain on his conduct, without a single stain on his action, is Che!"

Che has continued to have the most poignant and durable symbolic legacy of any revolutionary in history. Though he claimed to be thinking of global revolution to the end, Che was well aware of the personal legacy he was cultivating, even in the desolate final days in Bolivia. French intellectual Régis Debray, who was in Bolivia with Che and captured alongside him, later described the hardships they faced, including malnutrition, lack of water, absence of shoes, and only six blankets for 22 men. However, Debray claimed Che remained "optimistic about the future of Latin America" and was "resigned to die in the knowledge that his death would be a sort of renaissance."

Indeed, Che died at the age of 39, but his legacy is in its 45th year and shows no sign of dying anytime soon. If anything, the continued resonance of Che's legacy is attributable at least in part to the controversy over his life and work. As Che became the most iconic face of counterculture and revolution, more people tried to push back on romantic depictions of Che by pointing out that he was a cold-blooded executioner who was all too eager to deal violently with anyone he considered an opponent.

At the same time, Che would almost certainly consider it perverse that his face is now commonly found on the shirts of American college students, and that a photo of him is the most reproduced and recognizable photograph in history. As Isabel Hilton noted in *The New Statesman*, "Through the image, the complexities of Che's life and thought are reprocessed into an abstraction that can serve any cause. It has been painted as graffiti in Bethlehem, carried in demonstrations from Palestine to Mexico and borrowed by such artists as Pedro Meyer, Vik Muniz, Martin Parr and Annie Leibovitz. It has been used to represent causes as diverse as world trade, anti-Americanism, teenage rebellion and Latin American identity."

In essence, Che has become a malleable symbol that can mean different things to different people, all of whom form an opinion when they learn about his life and work. When everything's said and done, becoming a global symbol is an apt legacy for a man whose mission in life was to help the downtrodden people of the world.

Chapter 8: Cuba and the World

Throughout Castro's early period in power, Cubans disgruntled with the course the country had taken were permitted to emigrate at will (generally to the United States), a policy that would later change. This policy permitted the coalescence of a permanent and fierce opposition to Castro just 90 miles away in the Cuban exile center of Miami, Florida. In general, many of those who departed were members of the educated middle class, which was depriving the country of a competent managerial sector. It was in part due to this development that Soviet technicians and advisors were invited to live and work in Cuba during this period.

Meanwhile, in order to fulfill the basic promises he had made ever since Moncada, Castro made massive investments in public health, literacy, and education through the construction of a comprehensive welfare state, as well as massive infrastructure projects. These investments were enabled in part by the country's new arrangement with the Soviet Union, which would purchase an annual quota of sugar, making up for lost exports to the United States. The universalization of health services and education as well as sports programs and other public goods consolidated a general support for the Castro regime among sectors of the population previously excluded from access to the country's wealth.

There were exceptions to the general pro-Soviet direction the country took in the early post-revolutionary years. While Cuba's Soviet patrons would have preferred an unambitious foreign policy on the part of their client state that was closely aligned to Soviet strategic interests, Castro instead made a major investment in encouraging and supporting left-wing and anti-imperialist movements abroad.

Improbably, the small island state managed to make itself a major international political and cultural force. Che Guevara was a major driver of this tendency, convinced that the lessons of the Sierra Maestra campaign could be exported. In a period in which the Cuban Revolution was the rallying cry for a new generation of Latin American youth, it was not difficult to find recruits for guerrilla-style revolutionary wars against the many Batista-like dictators who held sway across the continent. Cuba attempted to help emergent revolutionary groups in Nicaragua, the Dominican Republic, Panama, Venezuela, Bolivia, Peru, and Argentina, and all of them were initially failures. Undeterred, Castro also turned his attention to Africa, where Cuba would end up playing a role in anti-colonial struggles in the Congo, Guinea-Bissau, Angola, and Mozambique. Castro also made important allies in Algeria and Tunisia. Cuban military involvement in Africa would continue into the 1970s in the form of support for left-wing governments or rebel groups. Castro discussed Cuba's involvement on the continent in an interview with Barbara Walters:

"The role of Cuba in Africa is mainly of a civilian nature, not of a military one. For a long time, we have been assisting a large number of countries, sending them technical assistance, especially doctors. On certain oc-casions, they have asked us for military advisers, to help organize their armed forces. And we have sent them, at the request of these governments. The case of Angola was the first occasion in which we sent military units. But we always had relations with the MPLA [Popular Movement for the Libera-tion of Angola] since they started their struggle for independence. And we assisted them. When they were at the point of achieving their independence an attempt was made to snatch it from them. The U.S. government invested some tens of millions of dollars to organize a movement, in Zaire, handled by the CIA. That is the famous FNLA [National Front for the Liberation of Angola]. The Portuguese organized another counterrevolutionary movement before they left-UNITA [the National Union for the Total Liberation of Angola]. South Africa was determined to stop the victory of the MPLA. We had been assisting them for a long time, and we were sending them weapons, and we had sent them some military instructors. We sent our first military unit at a time when the South African regular troops invaded Angola on October 23, 1975. Tank columns, artillery columns, blitzkrieg-type, Nazi-type, apartheid style. They sent their regular army. So we had to make a decision. Either we would sit idle, and South Africa would take over Angola, or we would make an effort to help. That was the moment. On November 5, we made the decision to send the first military unit to Angola to fight against the South African troops. That is the reason why we made the decision. If we would not have made that effort it is most probable that South Africa would have taken over Angola. We would also have Angola in the hands of the South African racists. I don't know what has been pub-lished in the United States about it, but I am sure that the American black people know the meaning of discrimination and of apartheid, and appreciate the effort we made. The American people, white or black, who understand apartheid will some day -- if they don't understand it today because they have not received the correct information -- he totally in agreement with us for the effort we made to save a black people of Africa."

A mural of Castro on a lighthouse in Angola

Castro even involved himself in U.S. affairs, making a particularly strong effort to develop relationships with African American militants of the Black Panther Party and like-minded organizations. Malcolm X personally met Fidel Castro in Harlem in September of 1960. Initially, Malcolm was merely part of a larger group of area leaders welcoming Castro to New York. But the Cuban leader had heard of the influential spokesperson for the Black Muslims and wanted to get to know Malcolm more. The two met for two hours, discussing racial liberation, and the meeting ended with an invitation for Malcolm to come to Cuba. The U.S. government took note and became more worried about both men. In the late 1960s and early 1970s, Castro also enjoyed high-profile visits from such figures as Stokely Carmichael and Angela Davis, and Cuba became a place of asylum for Black Panther leaders Huey Newton and Eldridge Cleaver. A second important role Castro's Cuba came to play internationally was as a regional cultural hub for Latin America.

Castro at the Lincoln Monument in Washington, D.C.

Through state cultural institutions such as the Casa de las Américas, the socialist government supported writers and other artists of a sympathetic bent from around the continent. In the 1960s, it seemed that everyone who was anyone in Latin America, including major novelists like Gabriel García Márquez, Mario Vargas Llosa, and Carlos Fuentes, spent a good deal of time in Havana.

By 1964, Americans were worried about the influence Cuba had not only in exercising foreign policy but as an example to other Latin American countries. Walter Lippman, the American writer who coined the phrase "Cold War", noted in 1964, "The greatest threat presented by Castro's Cuba is as an example to other Latin American states which are beset by poverty, corruption, feudalism, and plutocratic exploitation ... his influence in Latin America might be overwhelming and irresistible if, with Soviet help, he could establish in Cuba a Communist utopia."

However, the death of Che Guevara in October 1967 seemed to mark a turning point in post-revolutionary Cuba. His conviction that a small, determined band of fighters could once again be the spark that started a national revolution ultimately led him to Bolivia, where he ended up dying as a participant in an ill-fated struggle of this sort. Acknowledging Che's death nearly a week after, Castro delivered a eulogy of sorts, saying of Che, "If we wish to express what we want the men of future generations to be, we must say: Let them be like Che! If we wish to say how we want our children to be educated, we must say without hesitation: We want them to be educated in Che's spirit! If we want the model of a man, who does not belong to our times but to the future, I say from the depths of my heart that such a model, without a single stain on his conduct, without a single stain on his action, is Che!"

Guevara had been critical of Soviet influence on the island, and the importance of his personality and ideas had continued to limit Cuba's degree of subordination to Soviet policy. Once Guevara was gone, and once his death seemed to demonstrate the failed promise of continental Latin American revolution, Castro turned far more decisively in the Soviet direction. In 1968, he supported the Soviet military's brutal attack on the reformers of the Prague Spring, a move that was shocking to many who had viewed Castro as an independent voice within the communist bloc. In the same period, Castro oversaw a more thorough stamping out of lingering private enterprise in Cuba, extending state ownership and control to all areas of the economy. When questioned by Barbara Walters in the 1970s about confiscating private American property, Castro snapped back:

"It seems funny that you speak about the possibility of a country under economic blockade by the United States making any promise for indemnity of U.S. property. First of all, these properties recovered, in benefits, at least 10 times the investments made in Cuba before the triumph of the rev-olution. Second, the United States, through 18 years of hostility, aggression, subversive plans, and economic blockade, has brought about far worse damage in our country than the value of the properties that, as you say, were confiscated. So in that sense, we cannot make any gesture. I admit that on these questions of mutual economic interest and of mutual economic damages we could hold discussions in the future when the blockade against our country has ceased. On the air piracy agreement, we cannot forget that only a few months ago a Cuban plane was sabotaged while in fight; 73 people died, including the whole youth fencing team that had just obtained almost all the gold medals in an international match ... More than one million people accompanied the scarce re-mains of these victims to the burial place. That event that was perpetrated by people trained by the CIA, with the unquestionable complicity of the CIA, was the reason that we denounced the agreement ... How could our people understand, only a few months after that criminal act, and at a time when we still have no proof that the United States has made the decision to take measures against these terrorists, our signing this hijacking agreement ? We have said that as long as the economic blockade exists we will not sign this agreement ... We consider the economic blockade a serious act of hostility against our country, and it encourages terrorism. You blockade Cuba. On the other hand, you trade with South Africa; you make investments in a fascist country, a racist country, where 20 million blacks are discriminated against and oppressed."

There was also a strengthening of censorship, most famously exemplified by the arrest of poet Heberto Padilla, whose 1968 poem "Outside the Game" created a scandal for what seemed to be its open criticisms of the revolutionary state. Padilla's condemnation by the Cuban government became the first salvo in a war of words between Castro and an international group of writers and intellectuals who had been supporters of the Cuban Revolution. The latter condemned the restrictions on creative freedom, and Castro responded by calling them "despicable agents of cultural imperialism." The longstanding love affair with Castro and Cuba among left-leaning intellectuals had come to an end.

The issue of political prisoners has constantly been pressed against Cuba since the Revolution, and some have pointed to the fact Batista released Castro only to be overthrown by him as a potential reason Castro was harsh on political opponents. Castro dismissed that notion, telling Barbara Walters:

"Batista came to power by force, through a coup d'etat. He looted the country. All his acts were illegal. Our struggle against Batista's regime was totally just, and totally legal. What's more important, it was in agreement with the precepts of the constitution. I was as worthy of going to jail as Washington and Jefferson when they rose up against English domination in the old American colonies. And nobody questions the legitimacy, honor, and greatness of those American patriots who rose up against tyranny. And that is what we did. Batista was not the one who freed us; it was the people -- the masses with their demands that coin-cided with Batista's interest in an electoral masquerade. And he could not do it as long as we were in prison ... The CIA agents are men who, coming from a foreign country, worked to overthrow the revolutionary government, thus committing a very serious act ... We were doing something just. They were not doing anything just. We were serving our homeland. They were serving a powerful foreign power ... I do not consider myself a George Washington or a Thomas Jefferson ... I have never fought to occupy a position in history. I have always fought for concrete facts, for justice. I follow the slogan of Marti: All of the glory of the world fits in one grain of corn."

Chapter 9: Castro's Cuban Paradox

Castro speaking in Havana, 1978

The 1970s were a period in which Cuba became a Soviet satellite state, with Castro hewing closely to Soviet policy in most areas and making the economic support of the Soviet Union the linchpin of the Cuban economy. Although one of the fundamental goals of the Cuban Revolution had been to end Cuba's status as a massive sugar plantation for the wealthier nations to the north, it had instead settled on finding new customers. There were simple strategic reasons for this. The efforts of Che Guevara and others to diversify the economy had been for the most part a failure, resulting in austerity and rationing, and such developments weakened popular support for the government, further making a U.S.-sponsored attack in collaboration with exiled Cuban dissidents far more likely to win the support of the population. The most effective way for Castro's government to keep the country fed and clothed and still be able to fund the ambitious social programs that were the bedrock of the Revolution's popularity was to continue to do what Cuba had experience and infrastructure for: the growing and exporting of sugar.

By the mid- 1970s, the Cuban economy had stabilized into a period of 4% to 5% growth, a high number for Latin America in that period. This was the product not only of Soviet subsidies but of high international sugar prices. Castro again felt emboldened during this period to involve himself in foreign affairs, including military ventures into the continuing conflict in Angola and the newly Communist-aligned Ethiopia. A positive turn in foreign relations was the 1979 Sandinista Revolution in Nicaragua, which installed a pro-Cuban left-leaning regime in a country that had long been a U.S.-sponsored dictatorship.

However, a new crisis emerged in 1980, when a contingent of about 125,000 disgruntled Cubans fled to the United States in a dramatic fashion in what became known as the Mariel boatlift. This turn of events seemed to indicate a basic weakness in Castro's hold on power, just at the moments that the first signs of serious dissent were emerging in the Soviet bloc. On the other hand, Castro attempted to seize control of public relations by claiming that most of the Mariel refugees were criminals and lowlifes whom Cuba was glad to be rid of. Whatever the case, it seems that the mass exodus worked as an escape valve for some of the simmering discontent on the island.

The collapse of the Soviet Union in the late 1980s revealed the fragility of the economic order Castro had created, based as it was on one large economy for support. It also revealed the basic paradox of the revolution Castro had led; it had failed to make into reality what was probably its most important promise, genuine independence. Dependence had merely shifted from the United States to the Soviet Union.

Prior to the collapse of the Soviet Union, the Soviets purchased an annual quota of sugar from its Caribbean client state adding up to about $5 billion a year in revenue in the final years of their relationship. When the Soviet Union disbanded and abandoned its former ideological orientation, Cuba's sugar-based economy was a major casualty. Beyond the continuing United States embargo on the country's exports, cutting off access to the nearest large market, there was the more important problem that other countries, especially Brazil, had become far larger and more efficient growers and refiners of sugarcane in recent decades. Cuba's economy, as a consequence, contracted massively in the period 1990-1993, with GDP shrinking at an average rate above 10% during the entire period. Since most of its agricultural sector had been given over to sugar cane, it had relied for decades on discounted food imports from the Soviet bloc. Millions of Cubans were now threatened with starvation, and strict rationing was imposed.

Cuba was finally forced into economic independence, but because its economy was still oriented towards exports of sugar to large buyers, the experience of independence was by no means euphoric. It required the harsh austerity of the Special Period, and the strange ideological contortion of allowing capitalist development into Cuba in order to preserve its communist social order. Castro justified the Special Period by asserting, "We do not have a smidgen of capitalism or neo-liberalism. We are facing a world completely ruled by neo-liberalism and capitalism. This does not mean that we are going to surrender. It means that we have to adopt to the reality of that world. That is what we are doing, with great equanimity, without giving up our ideals, our goals. I ask you to have trust in what the government and party are doing. They are defending, to the last atom, socialist ideas, principles and goals."

In 1993, Castro announced and helped oversee a series of profound changes. First of all, the tourism and leisure industry, which had been a major feature of island life prior to the 1959 Revolution, would be revived on a massive scale. Second, and concomitantly, the U.S. dollar would be reintroduced as the major currency for foreign exchange and those elements of the service industry oriented toward foreign visitors. Third, the state industrialized sugarcane farms would be converted into autonomous agricultural cooperatives with the aim of greater alimentary self-sufficiency, allowing for the reintroduction of semi-private food markets as well. The first two of these changes were the most significant as far as the island's revolutionary identity went. Foreign hotel and resort chains were permitted to establish themselves, thus allowing for the first direct foreign investment in decades. The new legal dollar economy, associated with the tourist trade and with families who received remittances from relatives in the United States, created new inequalities, where individuals and families with access to dollars had access to foreign goods and luxuries closed off to most Cubans. Such possibilities incentivized the re-emergence of widespread prostitution directed mainly at foreign male visitors. By the mid-1990s, prostitutes in Havana were reported to be making over 10 times as much as university professors.

Despite the immense disruptions created by these changes, the basic ideological orientation of the Cuban state, as well as its commitment to provide free health care and education to its citizens, remained intact. By some accounts, the fact that ordinary Cubans had access to these basic goods even in the face of new inequalities of the Special Period may have weakened the appeal of full-scale capitalist reform. Beyond that, it is certainly the case that the silencing of dissent by imprisonment and other measures continued and continues to this day. Cuba has hundreds of political prisoners, down from the higher numbers of earlier times, but still a demonstration of lack of regard for free speech and free assembly.

Perhaps most surprising of all, the Cuban regime emerged from this set of painful transformations finally enjoying what it had ardently sought and failed to achieve in its early years: a strong network of alliances with like-minded governments around Latin America. Just when he seemed to have become a pariah on the world stage, Fidel Castro re-emerged as a friend and mentor to such leaders as Bolivia's Evo Morales, Ecuador's Rafael Correa, and especially Venezuela's late Hugo Chávez. The political trend in Latin America known as the "Pink Tide," which saw the rise of left-wing governments in Venezuela, Bolivia, Brazil, Argentina, Ecuador, and Nicaragua, removed the island from the political and commercial isolation it suffered after the demise of the Soviet Union. Under the sway of Chávez, a longtime admirer and friend of Fidel Castro, this new power bloc has provided Cuba with the kind of alliances and trading partners it needed. Meanwhile, nominally Communist but practically capitalist China has enjoyed positive relations with Havana in recent years and has generally benefited from the rise of a new Latin American left in its all-but-explicit endeavors to limit the global power of the United States.

Castro with Brazil's leftist President, Lula da Silva, in 2003

Perhaps the most surprising aspect of Castro's life is the way he relinquished power. In 2008, after a series of health problems, Fidel Castro stepped down from the presidency of Cuba, just short of his 50th anniversary at the helm of the Caribbean nation. There was an uneventful and unremarkable transfer of power to Fidel's brother Raúl, and things went on much as before, with the country retaining Communist rule under the same basic principles that had guided it since the early 1960s. Plenty of people had long anticipated that he would die in power, or he would be killed in power. In fact, Castro has long been thought of as a target for CIA assassination, to the extent that the American public is familiar with some of the various operations. One documentary detailed the over 600 ways the CIA allegedly concocted to assassinate Castro, including with an exploding cigar, exploding seashells near him on the beach, a mob gangland hit, and poisoning everything from his scuba suit to his fountain pen. Always suspicious of the CIA, Castro responded to a question by Barbara Walters about assassination attempts against him and answered:

"The problem is that the CIA has a budget of $5 million for espionage, murder, and sab-otage. It's a lot of money. The CIA uses more money each year than the total volume of Cuban exports, and you don't want us to think about the CIA. The CIA has made plans to assassinate the leaders of the revolution for more than 10 years, and you don't want me to think about the CIA. In fact, I am not the only one. Everybody here thinks about the CIA…

The CIA plans went on for more than 10 years, and I do not know when they ceased … At this very moment, I have no proof that the CIA has stopped its plans. I have not received any CIA message telling me that the plans have stopped, nor have we received any excuse from the U.S. government for the fact that the country's authorities for more than 10 years have been preparing the plans to assassinate the leaders of the revolution. In spite of the fact that the Senate investigated, and verified a very small part of those plans, never has any U.S. authority addressed the government of Cuba to apologize for these events…"

In the years since Fidel's retirement, he has remained a present figure but has stayed in the background much of the time. His brother's government has introduced a few piecemeal reforms that might be said to liberalize the country's economy, such as allowing Cubans to sell their cars and opening a wide range of small private enterprises. But these were far less significant than the market reforms implemented by Fidel himself in response to the exigencies of the 1990s. It seems, against all odds, that the small Communist state has undergone and survived a long series of existential crises, even including the resignation of the leader who had guided on its unusual path it for half a century.

These developments have been surprising to most observers abroad and probably many in Cuba as well. It had long been assumed that once Fidel Castro was gone, the Cuban political and economic experiment known as the Revolution was doomed. Foreign policy plans in the United States and beyond had been based on this assumption, figuring that even if Cuba was belligerent now, once it no longer had Castro to hold it together Communist rule would collapse and the country would fall inevitably back into the capitalist, U.S.-aligned column. The fundamental question of whether Cuban communism would survive once its supreme leader had disappeared seems to have already been answered.

Predictions about the country's future now seem to stand on shakier ground. It is true that Castro's symbolic presence still plays a role, and it remains to be seen what will happen in the event of his total disappearance, but the Cuban state has shown itself to be bigger than one man's personality. How long its current power arrangements will last in the long run is another question, but Cuba already has already changed significantly in economic terms over the past 20 years. It has also already survived a devastating threat to its current mode of government; Fidel and his government designated the hardship period that followed the withdrawal of Soviet support the "Special Period in Times of Peace," implying that while no war was underway, the country must respond to its latest exigencies as if under siege.

It is not clear to what extent the recent death of Hugo Chávez in Venezuela, which has provided discounted oil to Cuba under his leadership, will present a new challenge. What can be said with certainty is that even as Castro has retreated from public power, his vision for Cuba has essentially remained intact despite a wide array of internal and external threats to it. Castro's single-mindedness, ruthlessness, and charisma continue to pay him dividends through the survival of the system he imposed, even beyond his retirement.

Cuba's path has been unusual and unpredictable throughout its history. One of the few Spanish colonies that remained under imperial dominion until the end of the 19th century, it became a hotbed of nationalistic sentiment and a regional leader in modern Latin America. A semi-feudal slave economy through the late 19th century, within less than 100 years it became a pioneering socialist state looked to as a beacon by post-colonial regimes around the world. Castro's life path has been well-suited to the peculiar history of his country: an anti-communist nationalist who became a fervent communist, an agitator for regional autonomy who became a willing enforcer of the Moscow party line, a clear Soviet partisan who also held the presidency of the Non-Aligned Movement for several years, an ardent critic of capitalism who turned to international investors and resorted to chains to rescue Cuba's economy and his own rule from free-fall in the 1990s, an apparent dictator-for-life who stepped down well before anyone expected. Castro's forceful and often contradictory personality will continue to be an influence on Cuba and the world long after he and the political system he created have vanished.

Chapter 10: Che Guevara Quotes

Not surprisingly, people have taken a great interest in Che's writings, especially when so much of it was unearthed upon his capture and demise. Here is a list of some of Che's most memorable quotes:

"If you tremble with indignation at every injustice, then you are a comrade of mine."

"If any person has a good word for the previous government that is good enough for me to have him shot."

"In a revolution one wins or dies, if it is a real one."

"I have lived magnificent days."

"I am not interested in dry economic socialism. We are fighting against misery, but we are also fighting against alienation. One of the fundamental objectives of Marxism is to remove interest, the factor of individual interest, and gain, from people's psychological motivations. Marx was preoccupied both with economic factors and with their repercussions on the spirit. If communism isn't interested in this too, it may be a method of distributing goods, but it will never be a revolutionary way of life."

"Cruel leaders are replaced only to have new leaders turn cruel!"

"If they attack, we shall fight to the end. If the rockets had remained, we would have used them all and directed them against the very heart of the United States, including New York, in our defense against aggression. But we haven't got them, so we shall fight with what we've got." - Statement in an interview with a reporter for the London Daily Worker after the Cuban Missile Crisis.

"The university cannot be an ivory tower, far away from the society, removed from the practical accomplishments of the Revolution. If such an attitude is maintained, the university will continue giving our society lawyers that we do not need." Speech to university students, 1959

"War is always a struggle in which each contender tries to annihilate the other. Besides using force, they will have recourse to all possible tricks and stratagems to achieve the goal." - General Principles of Guerrilla Warfare

Much more definitive and much more lasting than all the gold that one can accumulate is the gratitude of a people. – Speech to the Cuban militia, 1960

"After graduation, due to special circumstances and perhaps also to my character, I began to travel throughout America, and I became acquainted with all of it. Except for Haiti and Santo Domingo, I have visited, to some extent, all the other Latin American countries. Because of the circumstances in which I traveled, first as a student and later as a doctor, I came into close contact with poverty, hunger and disease; with the inability to treat a child because of lack of money; with the stupefaction provoked by the continual hunger and punishment, to the point that a father can accept the loss of a son as an unimportant accident, as occurs often in the downtrodden classes of our American homeland. And I began to realize at that time that there were things that were almost as important to me as becoming famous for making a significant contribution to medical science: I wanted to help those people." - Speech to the Cuban militia, 1960

"We have to remind ourselves of this at every moment: that we are in a war, a cold war as they call it; a war where there is no front line, no continuous bombardment, but where the two adversaries — this tiny champion of the Caribbean and the immense imperialist hyena — are face to face and aware that one of them is going to end up dead in the fight." – Speech 3 weeks before the Bay of Pigs invasion

"On various occasions emissaries of the U.S. State Department came, disguised as reporters, to investigate our rustic revolution, yet they never found any trace of imminent danger. By the time the imperialists wanted to react — when they discovered that the group of inexperienced young men marching in triumph through the streets of Havana had a clear awareness of their political duty and an iron determination to carry out that duty — it was already too late." - 1961 speech

"Democracy is not compatible with financial oligarchy, with discrimination against Blacks and outrages by the Ku Klux Klan, or with the persecution that drove scientists like Oppenheimer from their posts, deprived the world for years of the marvelous voice of Paul Robeson, held prisoner in his own country, and sent the Rosenberg's to their deaths against the protests of a shocked world, including the appeals of many governments and of Pope Pius XII." - Speech to the ministerial meeting of the Inter-American Economic and Social Council (CIES), 1961

"Guerrilla warfare is a people's warfare; an attempt to carry out this type of war without the population's support is a prelude to inevitable disaster. – Guerrilla Warfare: A Method

"Mass struggle was utilized throughout the war by the Vietnamese communist party. It was used, first of all, because guerrilla warfare is one expression of the mass struggle. One cannot conceive of guerrilla war when it is isolated from the people. The guerrilla group is the numerically inferior vanguard of the great majority of the people, who have no weapons but express themselves through the vanguard." – People's War, People's Army

"The world is hungry but lacks the money to buy food; and paradoxically, in the underdeveloped world, in the world of the hungry, possible ways of expanding food production are discouraged in order to keep prices up, in order to be able to eat. This is the inexorable law of the philosophy of plunder, which must cease to be the rule in relations between peoples." – Speech before the U.N., 1964

"There are no borders in this struggle to the death. We cannot be indifferent to what happens anywhere in the world, because a victory by any country over imperialism is our victory, just as any country's defeat is a defeat for all of us." – Speech in Algiers, 1965

"For us there is no valid definition of socialism other than the abolition of the exploitation of one human being by another. As long as this has not been achieved, if we think we are in the stage of building socialism but instead of ending exploitation the work of suppressing it comes to a halt — or worse, is reversed — then we cannot even speak of building socialism." – Speech in Algiers, 1965

"In capitalist society individuals are controlled by a pitiless law usually beyond their comprehension. The alienated human specimen is tied to society as a whole by an invisible umbilical cord: the law of value. This law acts upon all aspects of one's life, shaping its course and destiny." - A letter to Carlos Quijano, editor of Marcha a radical weekly published in Montevideo, Uruguay; published as "From Algiers, for Marcha : The Cuban Revolution Today" 1965

"The road is long and full of difficulties. At times we wander from the path and must turn back; at other times we go too fast and separate ourselves from the masses; on occasions we go too slow and feel the hot breath of those treading on our heels. In our zeal as revolutionists we try to move ahead as fast as possible, clearing the way, but knowing we must draw our sustenance from the mass and that it can advance more rapidly only if we inspire it by our example." - A letter to Carlos Quijano, editor of Marcha a radical weekly published in Montevideo, Uruguay; published as "From Algiers, for Marcha : The Cuban Revolution Today" 1965

"At the risk of seeming ridiculous, let me say that the true revolutionary is guided by a great feeling of love. It is impossible to think of a genuine revolutionary lacking this quality. Perhaps it is one of the great dramas of the leader that he or she must combine a passionate spirit with a cold intelligence and make painful decisions without flinching. Our vanguard revolutionaries must idealize this love of the people, of the most sacred causes, and make it one and indivisible. They cannot descend, with small doses of daily affection, to the level where ordinary people put their love into practice." - A letter to Carlos Quijano, editor of Marcha a radical weekly published in Montevideo, Uruguay; published as "From Algiers, for Marcha : The Cuban Revolution Today" 1965

"Many will call me an adventurer, and that I am... only one of a different sort: one who risks his skin to prove his truths." – Letter to his parents, 1965

"Above all, try always to be able to feel deeply any injustice committed against any person in any part of the world. It is the most beautiful quality of a revolutionary." – Letter to his children to be read in the event of his death, 1965

"To die under the flag of Vietnam, of Venezuela, of Guatemala, of Laos, of Guinea, of Colombia, of Bolivia, of Brazil — to name only a few scenes of today's armed struggle — would be equally glorious and desirable for an American, an Asian, an African, even a European." - Message to the Tricontinental" sent from his jungle camp in Bolivia, 1967

"Each spilt drop of blood, in any country under whose flag one has not been born, is an experience passed on to those who survive, to be added later to the liberation struggle of his own country. And each nation liberated is a phase won in the battle for the liberation of one's own country." - Message to the Tricontinental" sent from his jungle camp in Bolivia, 1967

"Wherever death may surprise us, let it be welcome, provided that this, our battle cry, may have reached some receptive ear and another hand may be extended to wield our weapons and other men be ready to intone the funeral dirge with the staccato singing of the machine-guns and new battle cries of war and victory." - Message to the Tricontinental" sent from his jungle camp in Bolivia, 1967

Che Bibliography

Books About Che

Anderson, John Lee. *Che: A Revolutionary Life*. New York: Grove Press, 1997.

Bockman, Larry James. "The Spirit of Moncada: Fidel Castro's Rise to Power, 1953-1959." *GlobalSecurity.org*. Global Security, 1 April 1984. Web. 30 July 2012.

Castañeda, Jorge. *Compañero: The Life and Death of Che Guevara*. New York: Vintage, 1998.

James, Daniel, ed. *The Complete Bolivian Diaries of Che Guevara and Other Captured Documents*. New York: Stein and Day, 1969.

Books Fully or Partially Written by Che

A New Society: Reflections for Today's World,   Ocean Press, 1996

Back on the Road: A Journey Through Latin America,   Grove Press, 2002

Che Guevara, Cuba, and the Road to Socialism, Pathfinder Press, 1991

Che Guevara on Global Justice, Ocean Press (AU), 2002

Che Guevara: Radical Writings on Guerrilla Warfare, Politics and Revolution,   Filiquarian Publishing, 2006

Che Guevara Reader: Writings on Politics & Revolution,   Ocean Press, 2003

Che: The Diaries of Ernesto Che Guevara,   Ocean Press (AU), 2008

Congo Diary: The Story of Che Guevara's "Lost" Year in Africa   Ocean Press, 2011

Critical Notes on Political Economy: A Revolutionary Humanist Approach to Marxist Economics,   Ocean Press, 2008, ISBN 1-876175-55-9

Diary of a Combatant: From the Sierra Maestra to Santa Clara (Cuba: 1956–58)   Ocean Press, 2012

Episodes of the Cuban Revolutionary War, 1956–58,   Pathfinder Press (NY), 1996

Guerrilla Warfare: Authorized Edition,   Ocean Press, 2006, ISBN 1-920888-28-4

Latin America Diaries: The Sequel to The Motorcycle Diaries,   Ocean Press, 2011

Reminiscences of the Cuban Revolutionary War: Authorized Edition,   Ocean Press, 2005

Self Portrait Che Guevara, Ocean Press (AU), 2004

The Bolivian Diary of Ernesto Che Guevara,   Pathfinder Press, 1994

The Motorcycle Diaries: A Journey Around South America,   London: Verso, 1996

Castro Bibliography

Books About Castro

Benjamin, Jules R. (1992). The United States and the Origins of the Cuban Revolution: An Empire of Liberty in an Age of National Liberation. Princeton, New Jersey: Princeton University Press.

Bohning, Don (2005). The Castro Obsession: U.S. Covert Operations Against Cuba, 1959–1965. Washington, D.C.: Potomac Books, Inc.

Bourne, Peter G. (1986). Fidel: A Biography of Fidel Castro. New York City: Dodd, Mead & Company.

Coltman, Leycester (2003). The Real Fidel Castro. New Haven and London: Yale University Press.

Geyer, Georgie Anne (1991). Guerrilla Prince: The Untold Story of Fidel Castro. New York City: Little, Brown and Company.

Gott, Richard (2004). Cuba: A New History. New Haven and London: Yale University Press. ISBN

Quirk, Robert E. (1993). Fidel Castro. New York and London: W.W. Norton & Company.

Skierka, Volka (2006). Fidel Castro: A Biography. Cambridge: Polity.

Books Written Fully or Partially by Castro

Capitalism in Crisis: Globalization and World Politics Today, Ocean Press, 2000

Che: A Memoir, Ocean Press, 2005

Cuba at the Crossroads, Ocean Press, 1997

Nothing Can Stop the Course of History. New York: Pathfinder Press. 1986

Castro, Fidel; Ramonet, Ignacio (interviewer) (2009). My Life: A Spoken Autobiography. New York: Scribner. ISBN 978-1416562337.

Fidel Castro Reader, Ocean Press, 2007

Fidel & Religion: Conversations with Frei Betto on Marxism & Liberation Theology, Ocean